T0190816

DRAMA CLASS

The Drama Classics series aims to offer the world's greatest plays in affordable paperback editions for students, actors and theatregoers. The hallmarks of the series are accessible introductions, uncluttered texts and an overall theatrical perspective.

Given that readers may be encountering a particular play for the first time, the introduction seeks to fill in the theatrical/historical background and to outline the chief themes rather than concentrate on interpretational and textual analysis. Similarly the play-texts themselves are free of footnotes and other interpolations: instead there is an end-glossary of 'difficult' words and phrases.

The texts of the English-language plays in the series have been prepared taking full account of all existing scholarship. The foreign-language plays have been newly translated into a modern English that is both actable and accurate: many of the translators regularly have their work staged professionally.

Edited until his early death by Kenneth McLeish, the Drama Classics series continues with his aim of providing a first-class library of dramatic literature representing the best of world theatre.

Associate editors:
Professor Trevor R. Griffiths
Visiting Professor in Humanities, Universities of Essex and Hertfordshire
Dr Colin Counsell
School of Humanities, Arts and Languages, London Metropolitan University

DRAMA CLASSICS *the first hundred*

*The publishers welcome
suggestions for further titles*

DRAMA CLASSICS

THE SPANISH TRAGEDY

by
Thomas Kyd

edited and with an introduction by
Simon Trussler

NICK HERN BOOKS
London

www.nickhernbooks.demon.co.uk

A Drama Classic

This edition of *The Spanish Tragedy* first published in Great Britain as a paperback original in 1997 by Nick Hern Books Limited, 14 Larden Road, London W3 7ST

Reprinted 2002, 2005, 2010

Copyright in the introduction © 1997 Nick Hern Books Ltd

Copyright in this edition of the text © 1997 Simon Trussler

Typeset by Country Setting, Woodchurch, Kent TN26 3TB
Printed by CLE Print Ltd, St Ives, Cambs, PE27 3LE

A CIP catalogue record for this book is available from the British Library

ISBN 978 1 85459 377 1

Woodland
CARBON
www.woodlandcarbon.co.uk
NICK HERN BOOKS
Printed on Carbon Captured paper

Introduction

Thomas Kyd (1558-1594)

Thomas Kyd was born in London in 1558 and educated at the recently founded Merchant Taylors' School in the City, where he was a near-contemporary of the poet Spenser. One of the three known children of a well-to-do London scrivener – a copier of important documents, usually for legal purposes – Kyd apparently set out to follow his father's craft, but by 1583 may have been involved with the newly-formed Queen's company of players. In 1587 he seems to have entered the service of a noble household, variously identified as that of the Earl of Sussex or Lord Strange – each of whom lent his patronage to a theatrical troupe, for which Kyd, along with the young Christopher Marlowe, may well have written. He was evidently sharing lodgings or working quarters with Marlowe in the early 1590s, for when he was arrested and tortured on the orders of the Privy Council in May 1593 he accused his fellow dramatist of writing the 'vile heretical conceits denying the deity of Jesus' which were found among his papers. By the end of the month Kyd had been released – and Marlowe had met his death, allegedly in a tavern brawl. Kyd died little over a year later at the age of thirty-five, evidently a broken man. His parents survived him, but refused to administer his estate.

The Spanish Tragedy is the only extant play known to be of Kyd's original authorship, and even this attribution derives only from a reference in the dramatist Thomas Heywood's *Apology for Actors* in 1612 – though the writer Francis Meres included Kyd among 'our best for tragedy' in 1598. The common belief that he may have been the author of the so-called *Ur-Hamlet*, the lost play from which Shakespeare derived his own, is based on a sneering allusion by Thomas Nashe in 1589, while a 'prequel' to *The Spanish Tragedy*, *The First Part of Jeronimo*, would seem to have been written after

Kyd's death. In the very year of his death a translation from the
French of the tragedy *Cornelia* did appear under his name, and he
may also have written the full-length version of *Soliman and Perseda*
(the 'play within the play' in *The Spanish Tragedy*) which was published anonymously *c.* 1592. Around the same time the papers of
the manager Philip Henslowe refer to a *Spanish Comedy*, now lost,
and Kyd was possibly one of the authors of the anonymous
'domestic tragedy' *Arden of Faversham*. He may even have had a
hand in Shakespeare's *Titus Andronicus:* but the extent and nature
of his dramatic output remain as elusive as the details of his life.

What Happens in the Play

In the outer play, which 'frames' the action of *The Spanish Tragedy*
and serves as a Chorus between the acts, the Spanish nobleman
Don Andrea appears with Revenge – in whose custody he has been
placed by the guardians of the underworld, who cannot agree his
fate in Hell. Andrea has been slain in battle by Don Balthazar, the
heir to the Portuguese throne: and Revenge assures him that he is
to witness the vengeance of his mistress Bel-imperia – daughter of
the Spanish King's brother, the Duke of Castile – now that
Balthazar is a prisoner of the victorious Spaniards.

At the Spanish Court, the custody of Balthazar is disputed between
his joint captors – Bel-imperia's brother Don Lorenzo, and Horatio,
son of Hieronimo, the Knight Marshal of Spain. The King
recognises Horatio's claim to ransom, but places Balthazar in the
care of the more nobly-born Lorenzo. Balthazar sets out to woo
Bel-imperia, and the match is favoured for diplomatic reasons by
the King: but Bel-imperia makes plain her preference for Horatio,
not only as her lover but as avenger of the death of Andrea, whose
last rites Horatio performed.

At dagger's point, Lorenzo forces Bel-imperia's servant Pedringano
to betray the lovers' plans. In company with Balthazar and his
servant Serberine, they interrupt a midnight assignation in
Hieronimo's garden, hang up Horatio in the arbour and stab him
to death, then carry off the watching Bel-imperia as she pleads for

help. Hieronimo and his wife Isabella, aroused by the clamour, discover their dead son and lament his death. Hieronimo vows vengeance upon the murderers.

In Portugal, the Viceroy has dreamt that his son is dead, and has therefore believed the claims of the villainous Villuppo that Balthazar was treacherously slain by Alexandro – but the innocent man is rescued from execution when the returning Ambassador reports that Balthazar is held honourably captive. Back in Spain, Hieronimo discovers a letter written in blood in which Bel-imperia names Horatio's murderers – but their high rank forces him to proceed with caution. Even so, his enquiries after Bel-imperia arouse the suspicions of Lorenzo, who for greater security orders Pedringano to slay Serberine – and alerts the Watch so that the murder is observed and Pedringano condemned to be hanged. However, an intercepted letter to Lorenzo from Pedringano, falsely assured of a reprieve, confirms Hieronimo's suspicions.

Bel-imperia, appearing to believe her brother's explanation that he has only been acting to protect her honour, is allowed to return to Court, where Hieronimo's increasingly erratic behaviour, and his grief at his wife's madness and eventual suicide, make it easy for Lorenzo to prevent the old man from taking his accusations to the King. Lorenzo explains away his behaviour to Castile, who effects an apparent reconciliation between Hieronimo and his son. In the framing action, Andrea expresses his fury that the match between Balthazar and Bel-imperia is to proceed: but Revenge conjures up a dumb-show which portrays an imminently bloody outcome.

At last alone with Hieronimo, Bel-imperia rebukes him for his inaction, but the old man reassures her that he only awaits his opportunity – which presents itself when he is asked to stage a tragedy of his own writing for the wedding celebrations. Hieronimo persuades both Lorenzo and Balthazar to take part in the perform-ance, during which Bel-imperia's character slays Balthazar's and then takes her own life, while Hieronimo kills Lorenzo. He then reveals that the deaths have been not play-acting but real, and explains the full course of his actions over the body of his son. Prevented from hanging himself, he first bites out his tongue, then succeeds in taking his own life with a knife he is given to sharpen a quill for his confession. In the final Chorus, a satisfied Andrea plots the futures of his dead friends and enemies in hell.

The Theatres, the Texts – and the 'Additions'

The enduring popularity of *The Spanish Tragedy* in print – it went through ten editions between the first of 1592 (on which our own is based) and the last before the Civil Wars in 1633 – was almost certainly complemented by continuing performance in the theatre. The date and circumstances of the earliest stagings are uncertain, reflecting the sparsity of our knowledge of theatrical affairs until, following the closure in 1593 of all the theatres on account of the plague, the Chamberlain's and the Admiral's Men emerged to begin their long struggle for supremacy.

When Henslowe first mentions performances of the play, in 1592, these were by Strange's Men at the Rose Theatre, on the South Bank of the Thames – its foundations only recently rediscovered. Strange's are known also to have performed at the Theatre, the first permanent playhouse in London, built in 1576 in the northern 'theatre district' around Shoreditch, and at the Cross Keys, one of the surviving innyard theatres – the only permissible playing places inside the City walls. The Admiral's Men – who in 1600 moved from the Rose to the newly-built Fortune in Finsbury – inherited Strange's plays, but contemporary anecdotage has it that Richard Burbage, leading actor of the Chamberlain's company, also played Hieronimo: if so, this would probably have been at the Globe in Southwark, where the company moved from the Theatre in 1599.

All these were open-air, or 'public' theatres, in which the raised thrust stage was surrounded by a standing pit audience on three sides, while tiers of galleries around the perimeter provided better-off spectators with seating and some shelter. Above the stage, the gallery also served as a 'balcony' or higher performing area – or a 'window' such as Bel-Imperia speaks from in III, ix – while the cellarage below would have allowed access from the 'underworld', as for Andrea and Revenge There was also a curtained-off space in the back wall of the stage: this is thought to have been mainly used for characters 'discovered' (rather than making entrances) at the start of a scene, and it is probably such a curtain that Hieronimo 'knocks up' in IV, iii – in this case so that his son's body may be concealed behind it for later revelation. The many such careful stage directions suggest Kyd's experience in exploiting the full potential of the playing space. The arbour in which Horatio meets his end was evidently among the relatively few properties kept to decorate the otherwise bare Elizabethan stage. Costumes, on the other hand, were often lavish, and opportunities were seized for spectacular display – these ranging in our play from masques and dumb-shows to Pedringano's hanging and the Spanish army's triumphal passage over the stage.

In 1601 the theatre manager Henslowe records payments to Ben Jonson to write 'additions' to *The Spanish Tragedy*. Henslowe was sparing with his cash, and despite critics' claims that the additional scenes (first printed in the edition of 1602) are not in Jonson's style, there seems no good reason to doubt his capacity for pastiche. In the most interesting of these 'Additions', a Painter is commissioned by Hieronimo to immortalise Horatio's mortality: and Hieronimo's plea for the picture to 'portray' his exclamation – 'Canst paint a doleful cry?' – realigns the relationship between the verbal and the visual in the way that the famous woodblock from the 1615 edition (reproduced preceding our own text) compresses past and present into an emblematic snapshot of elided moments.

The Iberian Connection

There is no basis in history for *The Spanish Tragedy*, nor even a known romance from which its plot might have been drawn: but two issues in the play – of arranged marriage, and of conflict in the Iberian peninsular – would have been close to the conscious-ness of Kyd's original audiences. The dynastic marriage between Ferdinand of Aragon and Isabella of Castile had given birth to early modern Spain in 1479; and another dynastic marriage – between Queen Mary of England and the man who was soon to become Philip II of Spain, in 1554 – might, but for Mary's early and childless death, have secured England's permanent return to the Catholic fold. Philip's dislike of Mary's successor, the protestant Elizabeth, was intensified by English support for the Netherlands in their struggle for independence from Spain, and by the raids of licensed English pirates upon Spanish treasure ships returning from the New World. Philip continued to support the Catholic cause in England – notably the claim to the throne of the Catholic Mary Queen of Scots, whose execution in 1587 for allegedly conspiring against Elizabeth precipitated more open conflict. By the end of the 1580s this conflict had been resolved, at least temporarily, with the defeat of the Spanish Armada – while at the start of the decade there had, as in *The Spanish Tragedy*, been war between Spain and Portugal, with Philip sending an army to Lisbon successfully to assert his claim to the Portuguese throne. Following this, the two nations continued to share a monarch until 1640 – their resources stretched but their wealth mightily enhanced since the Pope had assigned them the joint right to carve up the Americas, in the year of Columbus's voyage of 1492.

Thus, at whatever time during the 1580s *The Spanish Tragedy* may first have been staged, it would have been a topical play. And even where it appears to lack topicality it would have given chauvinistic satisfaction to English audiences – as in the case of the masques presented by Hieronimo at I, iv, 140-74, showing English victories over two Portuguese and one Spanish king. The moral smugly drawn by the Iberians is that even unlikely fortunes of war such as conquest by the small, far-away island of England must be honourably accepted: the inhabitants of that small, far-away island, now actively challenging Spanish supremacy in every arena, were meant to relish the irony.

The history in the play, though imaginary, is essentially medieval; and its values, though subverted, are those of medieval chivalry. Thus, the relationship of Portugal towards Spain is one of feudal obligation – a fealty against which Portugal has recently tried to rebel. But the Portuguese Viceroy (the title is significant – he is not himself a king) repents his defiance – thinking himself to have been punished by his son's death – and is ready to restore payment of the tribute which has been at issue. As during the 1580s, the two nations seem as one: that the action shows a rigged dynastic alliance destroyed and the whole political basis of Spanish power undermined was, of course, wishful thinking rather than accomplished history for English audiences of the 1580s.

Seneca, Neoclassicism and the Popular Theatre

The Roman dramatist Seneca provided a model for the rhetorical style as also to some extent for the tone and theme of *The Spanish Tragedy*. Combining a highly formal diction with a lingering over sensation which is none the less gruesome for being described rather than enacted, Seneca's tragedies were for Kyd and his contemporaries more accessible than the Greek originals on which almost all were based. The dramatists of Italy and France emulated Seneca's more formal qualities – believing, for example, that violence should be reported rather than displayed, and accepting the constraints of his formal five-act structure, interspersed with choruses. And when (shortly before his death fighting the Spanish in 1586) Sir Philip Sidney wrote his *Apology for Poetry*, it was just such a 'neoclassical' model that he commended to English dramatists.

The Countess of Pembroke, Sidney's sister and an active patron of the arts, duly set out to encourage an English Senecan school, and herself published a translation of the French dramatist Robert Garnier's *Marc Antoine* in 1592. But the few English dramatists who consistently tried to adopt a Senecan style – Fulke Greville, for example, and Samuel Daniel – were not regarded as of the first rank even in their own time, let alone our own. And although Kyd himself (probably in a last bid to recover noble patronage as he neared his death) translated another of Garnier's Senecan tragedies, *Cornélie*, his *Spanish Tragedy* is truer to the less pedantic 'Englishing' of Seneca which helped to woo audiences to the Elizabethan popular theatre.

Kyd follows Senecan structure by employing a chorus between the acts – but since he only requires three interventions by the chorus, he only writes four acts: and he recognises (whether instinctively or pragmatically) that even the choric characters need to be part of

the action as well as commentators upon it. His revenge theme is
blood-soaked indeed – but its dramatic interest lies in revealing the
human psyche through behaviour *in extremis* rather than in demon-
strating the virtues or fallibilities of a school of philosophy. And,
most important, while Kyd knows well the dramatic impact of
formal rhetoric, and deploys a formidable range of rhetorical
devices, he also recognises that *action*, violent or otherwise, needs
to be seen as well as described.

Seneca served as tutor to the young Nero, who later gave the writer
his patronage when he became Roman Emperor: and with an irony
of which both Kyd and the speaker are conscious, Hieronimo in
our play tells the doubtful Balthazar and Lorenzo that Nero offers
a precedent for princely participation in the drama – the precedent
being the substitution of condemned criminals for actors in plays
which called for murders or executions. We do not know whether
any of Seneca's ten extant tragedies were thus embellished –
indeed, some scholars argue that his were 'closet' dramas, intended
only for reading or recitation – but we do know that Seneca's life
was almost as full of sensation and intrigue as his plays. Finally
ordered to commit suicide for his part in an alleged conspiracy, he
is said to have stoically observed his impressions as the life's blood
flowed from his gashed wrists.

Language, Rhetoric and 'Presentational' Acting

Until *The Spanish Tragedy*, 'blank verse' – use of the unrhymed
iambic pentameter – was rare in the drama. The only notable
earlier example was *Gorboduc*, a theatrically leaden tragedy written
in 1562 by Thomas Sackville and Thomas Norton, which is remark-
able only for its pioneering use of what was to become the distinc-
tive idiom of Elizabethan drama. What Jonson called the 'mighty
line' of Marlowe is more generally accepted as the defining moment
for blank verse: but Kyd's probably earlier usage may be viewed as
all the more interesting if we remember that its occasional irregu-
larities, or sudden diversions into something closer to a balladic
style, are not deviations from a norm but *explorations* of a verse
form as yet uncertain on its feet (all five of them).

Blank verse gave Kyd the flexibility to make *The Spanish Tragedy* work successfully for a highly heterogeneous audience – full of rhetorical devices, classical references, Latin tags and political allusions for the more sophisticated spectators, but also the idiom for a thundering good thriller. Dutifully to label all the rhetorical figures used by Kyd would be tedious here, but we may note in just one exchange between Balthazar and Lorenzo, at II, i, 113-38, instances of *anastrophe* (calculated inversion of the expected order of words); *anadiplosis* (the use of a word in one line which is then taken up in the next); and *polyptoton* (the use of the same word in calculatedly different senses). The Elizabethans took their rhetoric seriously – it figured on their grammar school syllabuses – and always delighted in the forceful patterning of words, whether in a sermon at Paul's Cross, an academic disputation, or a legal tussle in Westminster Hall. Indeed, when Kyd was writing, the word 'acting' itself would have denoted the conventionalised gestures used in oratory rather than theatrical 'playing': and it was in large part due to his example that what we might call the 'interactive' potential of rhetoric in the drama began to be be appreciated.

In contrast with such earlier and 'purely' rhetorical Elizabethan tragedies as the plodding *Gorboduc* or the pseudo-historical *Locrine*, of uncertain authorship, *The Spanish Tragedy* is, then, virtually the first play in which the word-patterning of the rhetoric is clearly and consciously predicated upon action. As developed by Kyd's successors, it was this fusion of quite formal verse with fluidity of structure and action which made for the distinct and self-sufficient art form that was the Elizabethan drama. Consider, for example, the balance Kyd strikes in the play between long set speeches, passages of more fluid, colloquial dialogue, and such recognisably 'rhetorical' but now theatrically pertinent speech patterns as *stichomythia* (exchanges in alternating single lines). Observe how Kyd 'stakes out' the exchanges in II, i, or III, ii, between formal speeches or soliloquies. Or explore the workings of the scene between Bel-imperia and Horatio at II, iv, 34-49, where the style and tone have the formality of a dramatised sonnet (such as Shakespeare was shortly to give Romeo and Juliet), but almost every phrase presumes, indeed *requires*, its appropriate and reciprocating action – possibly employing stylised conventions our own naturalistically-trained actors might find uncomfortable, but *action* none the less. Even the choric exchanges have their colloquial moments which make for movement – as when Andrea rebukes Revenge for nodding off to sleep in III, xiv.

The critic Robert Weimann suggested that in *The Spanish Tragedy* for the first time 'the monologue is no longer a static form of utterance: it does not express previously established facts or opinions. Rather, it represents the *process* of thinking and perceiving by which means the character . . . acts and changes in the context of the world of the play.' This is a perceptive comment: but for the actor it should not presume the need for a *psychological* rendering of the 'process of thinking', any more than he or she needs to seek a supposedly more 'primitive' mode. Consider the Viceroy's speech in I, iii, which *externalises* his own intense emotions at the supposed death of his son – while the chief villains of the piece are characterised (and their characters distinguished one from another) through rhetorical self-definition rather than an inner-directed exploration of emotions. By contrast with the more manipulative and pro-active Lorenzo, Balthazar's somewhat passive role is thus 'presented' through his greater rhetorical self-indulgence – as in his response to Bel-imperia's rejection early in II, i.

Among Kyd's other updatings of Senecan devices, the various 'reporting' scenes do not here serve (at least not often and not primarily) to keep blood and carnage off the stage, but rather to dramatise the variability (or, in Villuppo's case, the calculated fallibility) of points of view. This is not dissimilar to the method used by Pinter in, say, *Old Times* – another example of the way that *The Spanish Tragedy* now speaks to us across the naturalistic divide, like the many other Elizabethan and Jacobean plays that have been reclaimed for the live theatrical repertory since the 1970s. In part this is because the issues with which they are concerned continue to engage us today: but it is also because we have learned to be more open to non-naturalistic – as also indeed to non-Shakespearean – modes of performance.

The Political Economy of Justice and Revenge

The poet Ted Hughes, justifying his preference for Seneca's *Oedipus Tyrannus* over Sophocles' original, remarked that Seneca's characters 'are Greek only by convention: by nature . . . they are a spider people, scuttling among hot stones.' The image, we might feel, speaks as much of contemporary society as of Roman. And while I would take issue with Michael Hattaway's claim that *The Spanish Tragedy* 'occupied the collective consciousness of the Elizabethans in the way that the James Bond films did for a much later generation', this is not to dispute his recognition of the play's pre-eminent place in the popular culture of its age. But I would suggest that Kyd's play has its roots in an altogether rougher-edged variation on 'reality' than the fantasy world of James Bond – closer in contemporary popular culture to the world of the television soap opera *East Enders*, whose characters, as I write this introduction, are divided between condemnation and support for a father who, believing his daughter to be a rape victim, has taken justice into his own hands and exacted . . . revenge.

Now *The Spanish Tragedy* is not simply a 'revenge play', a label imposed upon it by later critics, any more than *East Enders* is a 'revenge soap'. Revenge *is* an important theme in the play, but not quite according to the conventional wisdom – which would have it that the vogue for revenge tragedy (with ours generally named as the first) sprang from an interaction of tensions in Elizabethan society: between a sense of personal honour, the biblical injunction that vengeance is a matter for God, and the increasing need of a newly-forged nation state to sustain a legal system independent of the old feudal loyalties. But 'honour', whence the desire for revenge supposedly springs, is subject to historical change: and in Kyd's society the late-medieval concept of honour as disinterested service to an overlord or mistress had been warped by the individualism of the Renaissance – to be redefined, with the dawning of the age of the duel, as an affront to one's machismo or sense of self-worth.

Since Andrea's death was in battle, his desire for revenge, which sets the whole play in motion, is ignoble and indefensible according to the laws of chivalry which ostensibly rule in Kyd's version of medieval Spain – but entirely reasonable according to the political economy of revenge in Elizabethan England. Thus, as David Margolies has pointed out, in *Henry IV, Part One* Shakespeare's Prince Hal appears to believe that he can *acquire* Hotspur's already unduly personal sense of honour by killing him in battle, as if he were making a takeover bid. Poised in the same historical no man's land between the Battle of Shrewsbury and the stage of an Elizabethan theatre, no wonder that Falstaff, asking 'What is honour?' could only declare it a word – a word whose definition, moreover, depended not only on one's historical moment but on one's social standing.

The Italian neoclassical critic Castelvetro (in his commentary on Aristotle's *Poetics*, published in 1570) was quite clear about this: only characters of noble birth would 'refuse to take legal action against the offender, nor do they bear the injury patiently, but they make their own judgements and kill in vendettas' – whereas the 'men of little courage' who are 'accustomed to obey the magistrates . . . make their supplications to officials who give them restitution and amends for their injuries through the law.' So it is surely well calculated on Kyd's part that his avenger by default, Hieronimo, is both a 'little' man and himself a magistrate: as Marshal of Spain, he is praised by others for his scrupulous fairness in dispensing justice to supplicants, yet when he himself needs to make supplication, the power and influence of his adversaries stand in his way. What drives him mad is not the murder of his son, but the impossibility of achieving justice through the due processes of law.

What the play's opening scene promises to be the vicarious revenge of Andrea upon Balthazar turns out to entrap in a web of retribution Andrea's allies and foes alike – his closest friend and his mistress, even those with whom he has little concern, such as those wretched servants complicit in Horatio's death. Indeed, the fates of Serberine and Pedringano – 'set up', as we might say, to take the blame for crimes planned and jointly committed by their 'betters'– serve again to highlight the impress of social standing upon justice. The pair act partly out of obedience to those who hold power, partly out of greed for gold – like Villuppo in the Portuguese Court, whose deception serves as little purpose to the action as to himself if not to emphasise the economic imperatives which weigh upon those who cannot afford 'honour'.

The Spanish Tragedy dramatises the idea and the enactment of revenge with a resonance that reaches beyond ethical quibbles into the heart of the inequalities and injustices of Elizabethan society. Aptly, perhaps, its conclusion sees not the restoration, however perfunctory, of some semblance of social order, but the implosion of the society that occupies the inner play – while Andrea's final line anticipates not Aristotelian catharsis but a cycle of Beckettian despair in that bleakly confident cry, 'I'll then begin their endless tragedy.'

'Hieronimo is Mad Again'

If we compare the title of Kyd's play with those of Marlowe or Shakespeare, we notice at once that this is not *The Tragedy of Hieronimo* but *The Spanish Tragedy* – its concern less with the fate of one man than of a whole society. Yet Elizabethan allusions privilege Hieronimo's name, and it is his character which led to so much imitation, variation, and eventual ridicule by Kyd's successors. For a tragic hero, however, he lacks the nobility expected of the type: so far from being a prince, he does not even enjoy the status of diplomat or ambassador, and in great affairs of state he has no voice: though evidently respected, he is confined to his legal brief. His son Horatio shares his equivocal status. Recognised for his martial bravery, he is given his economic due, but kept in his place by being denied the custody of Balthazar.

Hieronimo's vacillation over revenge is partly due, like Hamlet's, to his quest for certainty, but much more to his awareness of the superior social standing of his adversaries. He is an outsider and has no confidant – it would be unhistorical to expect a mere wife to fulfil that role – and he is therefore driven to introverted reflection. But Kyd keeps even his inner musings dramatic, requiring Hieronimo always to *act out* his soliloquies – most famously in the discovery of his murdered son in II, v, but twice, also, when he has to combine the reading out of letters with reacting to them.

Hieronimo increases his own isolation by either 'being mad' or 'acting' madness (it is for each actor to decide) – as when he takes a cue from one of his petitioners in III, xii, to launch into a monologue that remains rhetorically powerful while also psychologically 'presenting' his obsessive state of mind. The character's importance in the history of Elizabethan and later drama lies both in the need for the actor to find a way of thus 'presenting' psychological truth within a rhetorical mode, and in Hieronimo's own truth to the social and economic realities of his time. In this respect, perhaps it is no coincidence that the man who directs dumb-shows in the course of a play that is already set within a play finally strikes himself dumb – managing after all not to reveal 'the thing which I have vow'd inviolate'. He has, has he not, told all there is to tell already? Perhaps other truths are too subversive for a mere character in a play. The rest, as another revenger, Hamlet, was to reflect to another Horatio with his dying breath, is silence.

The Multiple Worlds of The Spanish Tragedy

The Spanish Tragedy looks back to the late-medieval preoccupation with the imminence of mortality, of which the grisly 'dance of death' was emblematic. But it looks forwards, too – with the feeling (more typically Jacobean than Elizabethan) of each human being's ultimate isolation, of the self-interest which (as Machiavelli had anticipated) lay behind most human actions, and of the impotence of the poor or justly discontented before the power of princes. Somewhere in the subtext, too, lie the equivocations of a newly protestant nation towards old supernatural forces. Here, they are made respectably classical in Andrea's underworld, but in Shakespeare's *Hamlet* they are more clearly Catholic in nature – for the Purgatory whence Hamlet's father claims to come had supposedly been abolished by the protestants.

The Calvinists, in proclaiming predestination, gave a religious gloss to an older determinism which saw man's destiny as controlled by Fate. And one of the reasons why drama, of all the arts, came to play so central a part in the life of late Elizabethan and Jacobean England was because theatricalisation – the age's perception of the 'great theatre of the world' – expressed humankind's own sense of a predetermined script being acted out, with God, or Fate, as its author and stage manager. *The Spanish Tragedy* both anticipated and formatively influenced this concern – and especially the pleasure of juggling multiple levels of dramatic reality. Even the full-length version of *Soliman and Perseda* (its theme miniaturised in the last act of *The Spanish Tragedy*) was thus to have its 'framing' action, in which Fortune, Love and Death debate their allegorised attributes.

In *The Spanish Tragedy* the multi-levelled working of the play is far more complex. Andrea and Revenge in the outer play observe and comment on the action of the 'tragedy' – the closing word of the first scene as it is of the last. This frames a main action which is glimpsed, we are told, through the visionary Gates of Horn – in such terms anticipating Pirandello by becoming a dream in Andrea's mind. And this main action is itself interspersed with the dumb-shows and play-within-the-inner-play stage-managed by Hieronimo. At other times characters on the same level take spectators' roles, as when Lorenzo and Balthazar observe Horatio and Bel-imperia making their foredoomed plans – or interpolate an additional layer of illusion, as when Revenge conjures his own dumb-show for Andrea, by way of predicting what is to follow.

We have no means of knowing whether these two observers were omnipresent, and the choice is of course the director's. But if, as the stage directions seem to assume, they *were* continuously on stage, the 'real' theatre audience would on occasion have been watching this pair from the underworld watching (or dreaming) a tragedy, whose characters were either spying on the actions of their fellows or serving as audience for yet further levels of buried action. When the last of these, the multilingual play of *Soliman and Perseda*, bursts its boundaries to make a mortal actuality of pretence, we might well feel confused about what is 'actuality' and what 'pretence'.

Besides this set of Chinese boxes of which he constructs his play, Kyd presents us with a real box as a stage property – the box falsely said to hold Pedringano's pardon. The scene of gallows humour in which the condemned man jests in full confidence of a reprieve is at one level an emblematic and literal presentation of 'empty' promises: but at another (as James Shapiro points out) it parodies the public execution of a criminal. When Alexandro is sent for torture and tied to the stake for burning, his sentence travesties that imposed on witches and heretics – while Horatio, symbolically disembowelled as he hangs, dies the death usually reserved for traitors, as suffered in 1586 by the conspirators in the Babington Plot. Because such demonstrations of state power were at one level public 'shows', to parody them in another kind of 'show' was to challenge that power – not once but thrice. Amidst the plentiful stabbings, shootings, and poisonings of later Elizabethan and Jacobean tragedy, such a challenge has no parallel.

In all this there is no infringing of the boundary between actors and audience – no direct address, like Richard III's, to a complicit crowd, or even the more oblique acquiesence of a Hamlet in sharing his thoughts with the spectators. Yet the connections between theatricality and real life could be more bizarre than such meta-theatrical mergings: and it is quite possible that, in May 1593, a troupe of strolling players – with, so Dekker claimed, Ben Jonson playing Hieronimo – were touring *The Spanish Tragedy*, even as Kyd was threatened with the tortures he had imagined for Alexandro, and feared a death like Horatio's.

A Note on the Text

The following text of *The Spanish Tragedy* is based on that of the first edition of 1592. In accordance with series style, Kyd's spelling has been modernised, except where mispronunciation might result, but I have elected largely to follow his original punctuation, which reflects rhetorical rather than grammatical usage – its pointing thus helpful to the actor in suggesting speech rhythms and pauses for thought or breath. I have only sparingly supplemented Kyd's already full stage directions, such editorial interventions being indicated by the use of square brackets.

Simon Trussler, 1997

Thomas Kyd: Key Dates

1558	Born, son of Francis Kyd, a London scrivener.
1565	Entered Merchant Taylors' School in the City of London.
1583-85	*c.* Possibly a member of the Queen's company of players.
1585-89	*c.* Probable limits for the first performance of *The Spanish Tragedy.*
1588	Publication of a translation by 'T.K.' of Tasso's prose treatise on domestic virtues, *Il padre di famiglia*, as *The Householder's Philosophy.* Kyd by now conjecturally in the service of a noble household.
1589	Nashe's preface to Greene's *Menaphon* offers allusive evidence of Kyd's authorship of an early, lost version of *Hamlet.*
1591	Mention of a *Spanish Comedy* in the papers of Philip Henslowe.
1592	*c.* Publication, anonymously, of *Soliman and Perseda*, and of the first of the ten extant contemporary editions of *The Spanish Tragedy*. First recorded performance of *The Spanish Tragedy* by Strange's Men at the Rose.
1593	May, Kyd arrested for heresy and tortured on the orders of the Privy Council. Published a translation of Robert Garnier's *Cornélie* from the French.
1594	August, died intestate. There is no record of his having married or had children.

For Further Reading

Philip Edwards's *Thomas Kyd and Early Elizabethan Tragedy* (London: Longmans, 1966) provides a helpful but very brief context for our author. The only biographical study – which acknowledges its limitations in its title – is Arthur Freeman's *Thomas Kyd: Facts and Problems* (Oxford: Clarendon Press, 1967). Peter B. Murray's *Thomas Kyd* (New York: Twayne, 1969) largely confines itself to *The Spanish Tragedy*, and there are helpful introductions in three scholarly editions which also provide full annotation and textual apparatus: the 'Revels Plays' edition, ed. Philip Edwards (London: Methuen, 1959); the old-spelling edition in the 'Fountainwell Drama Texts' series, ed. Thomas W. Ross (Edinburgh: Oliver and Boyd, 1968); and the 'New Mermaid' edition, ed. J.R. Mulryne (London: Black, 1989). The standard but long outdated work on the genre of our play is Fredson Bowers's *English Revenge Tragedy* (Princeton University Press, 1940).

The chapter on Kyd in Wolfgang Clemen's lucid but essentially academic exploration of the development of the 'set speech' in *English Tragedy before Shakespeare* (London: Methuen, 1967) may usefully be complemented with the chapter on the rendering of the play's 'architectonic design' in the live theatre in Michael Hattaway's *Elizabethan Popular Theatre* (London: Routledge, 1982). Helpful articles on the play in collections are Jonas Barish's '*The Spanish Tragedy*, or the Pleasures and Perils of Rhetoric', in *Elizabethan Theatre*, ed. John Russell Brown and Bernard Harris (London: Arnold, 1966), and James Shapiro's 'Tragedies Naturally Performed: Kyd's Representation of Violence', in *Staging the Renaissance*, ed. David Scott Kastan and Peter Stallybrass (London: Routledge, 1991).

THE SPANISH TRAGEDY

Dramatis Personae

GHOST *of Don Andrea*
REVENGE
KING *of Spain*
CYPRIAN, *Duke of Castile, his brother*
LORENZO, *son to Castile*
BEL-IMPERIA, *sister to Lorenzo*
GENERAL *of the Spanish Army*
VICEROY *of Portingale*
PEDRO, *brother to the Viceroy*
PRINCE BALTHAZAR, *son to the Viceroy*
ALEXANDRO, *a nobleman of Portingale*
VILLUPPO, *a nobleman of Portingale*
AMBASSADOR *from Portingale to Spain*
HIERONIMO, *Knight Marshal of Spain*
ISABELLA, *wife to Hieronimo*
HORATIO, *son to Hieronimo and Isabella*
PEDRINGANO, *servant to Bel-imperia*
SERBERINE, *servant to Prince Balthazar*
CHRISTOPHIL, *servant to Don Lorenzo*
BAZULTO, *an old man*

Page *to Lorenzo*, General, Deputy, Watchmen, Hangman,
Maid to Isabella, Two Portuguese, Servant, Three Citizens,
Portuguese Nobles, Soldiers, Officers, Attendants, Halberdiers

Three Knights, Three Kings, Drummer, Hymen, and Two
Torch-Bearers *in the dumb-shows*

PEDRO *and* JAQUES, *servants to Hieronimo, and* BAZARDO,
a Painter, in the additional passages

Act I, Scene i

Enter the GHOST *of Andrea, and with him* REVENGE.

GHOST. When this eternal substance of my soul
　　Did live imprison'd in my wanton flesh:
　　Each in their function serving other's need,
　　I was a courtier in the Spanish Court.
　　My name was Don Andrea, my descent　　　　　　　　5
　　Though not ignoble, yet inferior far
　　To gracious fortunes of my tender youth:
　　For there in prime and pride of all my years,
　　By duteous service and deserving love,
　　In secret I possess'd a worthy dame,　　　　　　　　10
　　Which hight sweet Bel-imperia by name.
　　But in the harvest of my summer joys,
　　Death's winter nipp'd the blossoms of my bliss,
　　Forcing divorce betwixt my love and me.
　　For in the late conflict with Portingale,　　　　　　15
　　My valour drew me into danger's mouth,
　　Till life to death made passage through my wounds.
　　When I was slain, my soul descended straight,
　　To pass the flowing stream of Acheron:
　　But churlish Charon, only boatman there,　　　　　　20
　　Said that my rites of burial not perform'd,
　　I might not sit amongst his passengers.
　　Ere Sol had slept three nights in Thetis' lap
　　And slak'd his smoking chariot in her flood:
　　By Don Horatio our Knight Marshal's son,　　　　　　25
　　My funerals and obsequies were done.
　　Then was the ferryman of hell content
　　To pass me over to the slimy strond,
　　That leads to fell Avernus' ugly waves:
　　There pleasing Cerberus with honey'd speech,　　　　30

I pass'd the perils of the foremost porch.
Not far from hence amidst ten thousand souls,
Sat Minos, Aeacus, and Rhadamanth,
To whom no sooner 'gan I make approach,
To crave a passport for my wand'ring ghost: 35
But Minos in graven leaves of lottery,
Drew forth the manner of my life and death.
'This knight' (quoth he) 'both liv'd and died in love,
And for his love tried fortune of the wars,
And by war's fortune lost both love and life.'   40
'Why then,' said Aeacus, convey him hence,
To walk with lovers in our fields of love:
And spend the course of everlasting time,
Under green myrtle trees and cypress shades.'
'No, no,' said Rhadamanth, 'It were not well,   45
With loving souls to place a martialist:
He died in war, and must to martial fields:
Where wounded Hector lives in lasting pain,
And Achilles' myrmidons do scour the plain.'
Then Minos mildest censor of the three,   50
Made this device to end the difference.
'Send him' (quoth he) 'to our infernal King:
To doom him as best seems his majesty.'
To this effect my passport straight was drawn.
In keeping on my way to Pluto's court,   55
Through dreadful shades of ever-glooming night,
I saw more sights than thousand tongues can tell,
Or pens can write, or mortal hearts can think.
Three ways there were, that on the right hand side
Was ready way unto the foresaid fields,   60
Where lovers live, and bloody martialists,
But either sort contain'd within his bounds.
The left hand path declining fearfully,
Was ready downfall to the deepest hell,
Where bloody furies shakes their whips of steel,   65
And poor Ixion turns an endless wheel.
Where usurers are chok'd with melting gold,
And wantons are embrac'd with ugly snakes:

And murderers groan with never killing wounds,
And perjur'd wights scalded in boiling lead,   70
And all foul sins with torments overwhelm'd.
'Twixt these two ways, I trod the middle path,
Which brought me to the fair Elysian green.
In midst whereof there stands a stately tower,
The walls of brass, the gates of adamant.   75
Here finding Pluto with his Proserpine,
I show'd my passport humbled on my knee.
Whereat fair Proserpine began to smile,
And begg'd that only she might give my doom.
Pluto was pleas'd, and seal'd it with a kiss.   80
Forthwith (Revenge) she rounded thee in th' ear,
And bad thee lead me through the Gates of Horn,
Where dreams have passage in the silent night.
No sooner had she spoke but we were here,
I wot not how, in twinkling of an eye.   85

REVENGE. Then know Andrea that thou art arriv'd
Where thou shalt see the author of thy death,
Don Balthazar the Prince of Portingale,
Depriv'd of life by Bel-imperia:
Here sit we down to see the mystery,   90
And serve for Chorus in this tragedy.

Act I, Scene ii

Enter Spanish KING, GENERAL, CASTILE, HIERONIMO.

KING. Now say Lord General, how fares our camp?

GENERAL. All well my sovereign liege, except some few,
    That are deceas'd by fortune of the war.

KING. But what portends thy cheerful countenance,
    And posting to our presence thus in haste?   5
    Speak man, hath fortune given us victory?

GENERAL. Victory my liege, and that with little loss.

KING. Our Portingals will pay us tribute then.

GENERAL. Tribute and wonted homage therewithal.

KING. Then bless'd be heaven, and guider of the heavens,   10
    From whose fair influence such justice flows.

CASTILE. *O multum dilecte Deo, tibi militat aether,*
    Et conjuratae curvato poplito gentes
    Succumbunt: recti soror est victoria juris.

KING. Thanks to my loving brother of Castile.   15
    But General, unfold in brief discourse
    Your form of battle and your war's success,
    That adding all the pleasure of thy news
    Unto the height of former happiness,
    With deeper wage and greater dignity,   20
    We may reward thy blissful chivalry.

GENERAL. Where Spain and Portingale do jointly knit
    Their frontiers, leaning on each other's bound:
    There met our armies in their proud array,
    Both furnish'd well, both full of hope and fear: 25
    Both menacing alike with daring shows,
    Both vaunting sundry colours of device,
    Both cheerly sounding trumpets, drums and fifes.
    Both raising dreadful clamours to the sky,
    That valleys, hills, and rivers made rebound,   30
    And heaven itself was frighted with the sound.
    Our battles both were pitch'd in squadron form,
    Each corner strongly fenc'd with wings of shot,
    But ere we join'd and came to push of pike,
    I brought a squadron of our readiest shot,   35
    From out our rearward to begin the fight,
    They brought another wing to encounter us:
    Meanwhile our ord'nance play'd on either side,
    And captains strove to have their valours tried.
    Don Pedro their chief horsemen's corlonel,   40
    Did with his cornet bravely make attempt,
    To break the order of our battle ranks.
    But Don Rogero worthy man of war,

March'd forth against him with our musketeers,
And stopp'd the malice of his fell approach.   45
While they maintain hot skirmish to and fro,
Both battles join and fall to handy blows,
Their violent shot resembling th' ocean's rage,
When roaring loud and with a swelling tide,
It beats upon the rampiers of huge rocks,   50
And gapes to swallow neighbour bounding lands.
Now while Bellona rageth here and there,
Thick storms of bullets rain like winter's hail,
And shiver'd lances dark the troubled air.
Pede pes et cuspide cuspis,   55
Anni sonant annis, vir petiturque viro.
On every side drop captains to the ground,
And soldiers some ill maim'd, some slain outright:
Here falls a body scinder'd from his head,
There legs and arms lie bleeding on the grass,   60
Mingl'd with weapons and unbowelled steeds:
That scattering over spread the purple plain.
In all this turmoil three long hours and more,
The victory to neither part inclin'd,
Till Don Andrea with his brave launciers,   65
In their main battle made so great a breach,
That half dismay'd, the multitude retir'd:
But Balthazar the Portingales' young Prince,
Brought rescue and encourag'd them to stay:
Here-hence the fight was eagerly renew'd,   70
And in that conflict was Andrea slain,
Brave man at arms, but weak to Balthazar.
Yet while the Prince insulting over him,
Breath'd out proud vaunts, sounding to our reproach,
Friendship and hardy valour join'd in one,   75
Prick'd forth Horatio our Knight Marshal's son,
To challenge forth that Prince in single fight:
Not long between these twain the fight endur'd,
But straight the Prince was beaten from his horse,
And forc'd to yield him prisoner to his foe: 80
When he was taken, all the rest they fled,

And our carbines pursu'd them to the death,
Till, Phoebus waning to the western deep,
Our trumpeters were charg'd to sound retreat.

KING. Thanks good Lord General for these good news,   85
And for some argument of more to come,
Take this and wear it for thy sovereign's sake.

Give him his chain.

But tell me now, hast thou confirm'd a peace?

GENERAL. No peace my liege, but peace conditional,
That if with homage tribute be well paid,   90
The fury of your forces will be stay'd.
And to this peace their Viceroy hath subscrib'd.

Give the KING *a paper.*

And made a solemn vow that during life,
His tribute shall be truly paid to Spain.

KING. These words, these deeds, become thy person well.   95
But now Knight Marshal frolic with thy King,
For 'tis thy son that wins this battle's prize.

HIERONIMO. Long may he live to serve my sovereign liege,
And soon decay unless he serve my liege.

A tucket afar off.

KING. Nor thou nor he shall die without reward.   100
What means the warning of this trumpet's sound?

GENERAL. This tells me that your grace's men of war,
Such as war's fortune hath reserv'd from death,
Come marching on towards your royal seat,
To show themselves before your majesty,   105
For so I gave in charge at my depart.
Whereby by demonstration shall appear,
That all (except three hundred or few more)
Are safe return'd and by their foes enrich'd.

The ARMY *enters,* BALTHAZAR *between* LORENZO *and*
HORATIO *captive.*

KING. A gladsome sight, I long to see them here.   110

They enter and pass by.

Was that the warlike Prince of Portingale,
That by our nephew was in triumph led?

GENERAL. It was, my liege, the Prince of Portingale.

KING. But what was he that on the other side,
Held him by th' arm as partner of the prize?   115

HIERONIMO. That was my son my gracious sovereign,
Of whom, though from his tender infancy,
My loving thoughts did never hope but well.
He never pleas'd his father's eyes till now,
Nor fill'd my heart with overcloying joys.   120

KING. Go let them march once more about these walls,
That staying them we may confer and talk,
With our brave prisoner and his double guard.
Hieronimo, it greatly pleaseth us,
That in our victory thou have a share,   125
By virtue of thy worthy son's exploit.

Enter [the ARMY] *again.*

Bring hither the young Prince of Portingale,
The rest march on, but ere they be dismiss'd,
We will bestow on every soldier two ducats,
And on every leader ten, that they may know   130
Our largesse welcomes them.

Exeunt all but BALTHAZAR, LORENZO, HORATIO
[*and* KING].

Welcome Don Balthazar, welcome nephew,
And thou Horatio thou art welcome too:
Young Prince, although thy father's hard misdeeds,
In keeping back the tribute that he owes,   135
Deserve but evil measure at our hands:
Yet shalt thou know that Spain is honourable.

BALTHAZAR. The trespass that my father made in peace,
  Is now controll'd by fortune of the wars:
  And cards once dealt, it boots not ask why so,   140
  His men are slain, a weakening to his realm,
  His colours seiz'd, a blot unto his name,
  His son distress'd, a corsive to his heart,
  These punishments may clear his late offence.

KING. Ay Balthazar, if he observe this truce,   145
  Our peace will grow the stronger for these wars:
  Meanwhile live thou though not in liberty,
  Yet free from bearing any servile yoke.
  For in our hearing thy deserts were great,
  And in our sight thy self art gracious.   150

BALTHAZAR. And I shall study to deserve this grace.

KING. But tell me, for their holding makes me doubt,
  To which of these twain art thou prisoner?

LORENZO. To me my liege.

HORATIO.   To me my sovereign.

LORENZO. This hand first took his courser by the reins. 155

HORATIO. But first my lance did put him from his horse.

LORENZO. I seiz'd his weapon, and enjoy'd it first.

HORATIO. But first I forc'd him lay his weapons down.

KING. Let go his arm, upon our privilege.

  Let him go.

  Say worthy Prince, to whether didst thou yield?   160

BALTHAZAR. To him in courtesy, to this perforce:
  He spake me fair, this other gave me strokes:
  He promis'd life, this other threaten'd death:
  He won my love, this other conquer'd me:
  And truth to say I yield myself to both.   165

HIERONIMO. But that I know your grace for just and wise,
    And might seem partial in this difference,
    Enforc'd by nature and by law of arms,
    My tongue should plead for young Horatio's right.
    He hunted well that was a lion's death,   170
    Not he that in a garment wore his skin:
    So hares may pull dead lions by the beard.

KING. Content thee Marshal thou shalt have no wrong
    And for thy sake thy son shall want no right.
    Will both abide the censure of my doom?   175

LORENZO. I crave no better than your grace awards.

HORATIO. Nor I, although I sit beside my right.

KING. Then by my judgment thus your strife shall end,
    You both deserve and both shall have reward.
    Nephew, thou took'st his weapon and his horse,   180
    His weapons and his horse are thy reward.
    Horatio, thou didst force him first to yield,
    His ransom therefore is thy valour's fee:
    Appoint the sum as you shall both agree.
    But nephew thou shalt have the prince in guard,   185
    For thine estate best fitteth such a guest.
    Horatio's house were small for all his train,
    Yet in regard thy substance passeth his,
    And that just guerdon may befall desert,
    To him we yield the armour of the Prince.   190
    How likes Don Balthazar of this device?

BALTHAZAR. Right well my liege, if this proviso were,
    That Don Horatio bear us company,
    Whom I admire and love for chivalry.

KING. Horatio leave him not that loves thee so,   195
    Now let us hence to see our soldiers paid,
    And feast our prisoner as our friendly guest.

Exeunt.

Act I, Scene iii

Enter VICEROY, ALEXANDRO, VILLUPPO [*and*
ATTENDANTS].

VICEROY. Is our ambassador despatch'd for Spain?

ALEXANDRO. Two days (my liege) are pass'd since his depart.

VICEROY. And tribute payment gone along with him?

ALEXANDRO Ay my good lord.

VICEROY. Then rest we here awhile in our unrest,   5
    And feed our sorrows with some inward sighs,
    For deepest cares break never into tears.
    But wherefore sit I in a regal throne,
    This better fits a wretch's endless moan.
    Yet this is higher than my fortunes reach,   10
    And therefore better than my state deserves.

Falls to the ground.

    Ay, ay, this earth, image of melancholy,
    Seeks him whom fates adjudge to misery:
    Here let me lie, now am I at the lowest.
    Qui jacet in terra non habet unde cadat.   15
    In me consumpsit vires fortuna nocendo.
    Nil superest ut jam possit obesse magis.
    Yes, Fortune may bereave me of my crown:
    Here take it now, let Fortune do her worst,
    She will not rob me of this sable weed,   20
    O no, she envies none but pleasant things,
    Such is the folly of despiteful chance:
    Fortune is blind and sees not my deserts,
    So is she deaf and hears not my laments:
    And could she hear, yet is she wilful mad,   25
    And therefore will not pity my distress.
    Suppose that she could pity me, what then?
    What help can be expected at her hands?
    Whose foot is standing on a rolling stone,
    And mind more mutable than fickle winds.   30

Why wail I then where's hope of no redress?
O yes, complaining makes my grief seem less.
My late ambition hath distain'd my faith,
My breach of faith occasion'd bloody wars,
Those bloody wars have spent my treasure,   35
And with my treasure my people's blood,
And with their blood, my joy and best belov'd,
My best belov'd, my sweet and only son.
O wherefore went I not to war myself?
The cause was mine I might have died for both: 40
My years were mellow, his but young and green,
My death were natural, but his was forc'd.

ALEXANDRO. No doubt my liege but still the Prince survives.

VICEROY. Survives, ay where?

ALEXANDRO. In Spain, a prisoner by mischance of war.   45

VICEROY. Then they have slain him for his father's fault.

ALEXANDRO. That were a breach to common law of arms.

VICEROY. They reck no laws that meditate revenge.

ALEXANDRO. His ransom's worth will stay from foul revenge.

VICEROY. No, if he liv'd the news would soon be here.   50

ALEXANDRO. Nay evil news fly faster still than good.

VICEROY. Tell me no more of news, for he is dead.

VILLUPPO. My sovereign, pardon the author of ill news,
    And I'll bewray the fortune of thy son.

VICEROY. Speak on, I'll guerdon thee whate'er it be,   55
    Mine ear is ready to receive ill news,
    My heart grown hard 'gainst mischief's battery,
    Stand up I say and tell thy tale at large.

VILLUPPO. Then hear that truth which these mine eyes
      have seen.
    When both the armies were in battle join'd,   60
    Don Balthazar amidst the thickest troops,

To win renown did wondrous feats of arms:
Amongst the rest I saw him hand to hand
In single fight with their Lord General.
Till Alexandro that here counterfeits,   65
Under the colour of a duteous friend,
Discharg'd his pistol at the Prince's back,
As though he would have slain their General.
But therewithal Don Balthazar fell down:
And when he fell then we began to fly,   70
But had he liv'd the day had sure been ours.

ALEXANDRO. O wicked forgery: O traitorous miscreant.

VICEROY. Hold thou thy peace, but now Villuppo say,
    Where then became the carcass of my son?

VILLUPPO. I saw them drag it to the Spanish tents.   75

VICEROY. Ay, ay, my nightly dreams have told me this:
    Thou false, unkind, unthankful traitorous beast,
    Wherein had Balthazar offended thee,
    That thou shouldst thus betray him to our foes?
    Was 't Spanish gold that bleared so thine eyes,   80
    That thou couldst see no part of our deserts?
    Perchance because thou art Terceira's lord,
    Thou hadst some hope to wear this diadem,
    If first my son and then my self were slain:
    But thy ambitious thought shall break thy neck.   85
    Ay, this was it that made thee spill his blood,

Take the crown and put it on again.

    But I'll now wear it till thy blood be spilt.

ALEXANDRO. Vouchsafe (dread sovereign) to hear me speak.

VICEROY. Away with him, his sight is second hell,
    Keep him till we determine of his death.   90
    If Balthazar be dead, he shall not live.
    Villuppo, follow us for thy reward.

    Exit VICEROY [*and* ALEXANDRO, *guarded*].

VILLUPPO. Thus have I with an envious, forged tale,
    Deceived the king, betray'd mine enemy.
    And hope for guerdon of my villainy.   95

    Exit.

Act I, Scene iv

Enter HORATIO *and* BEL-IMPERIA.

BEL-IMPERIA. Signior Horatio, this is the place and hour,
    Wherein I must entreat thee to relate,
    The circumstance of Don Andrea's death:
    Who living was my garland's sweetest flower,
    And in his death hath buried my delights.   5

HORATIO. For love of him and service to your self,
    I nill refuse this heavy doleful charge.
    Yet tears and sighs, I fear will hinder me.
    When both our armies were enjoin'd in fight,
    Your worthy chevalier amidst the thick'st,   10
    For glorious cause still aiming at the fairest,
    Was at the last by young Don Balthazar,
    Encounter'd hand to hand: their fight was long,
    Their hearts were great, their clamours menacing,
    Their strength alike, their strokes both dangerous.   15
    But wrathful Nemesis that wicked power,
    Envying at Andrea's praise and worth,
    Cut short his life to end his praise and worth.
    She, she herself disguis'd in armour's mask,
    (As Pallas was before proud Pergamus)   20
    Brought in a fresh supply of halberdiers,
    Which paunch'd his horse and ding'd him to the ground.
    Then young Don Balthazar with ruthless rage,
    Taking advantage of his foe's distress,
    Did finish what his halberdiers begun,   25
    And left not till Andrea's life was done.
    Then, though too late incens'd with just remorse,

I with my band set forth against the Prince,
And brought him prisoner from his halberdiers.   29

BEL-IMPERIA. Would thou hadst slain him that so slew my love.
But then was Don Andrea's carcass lost?

HORATIO. No, that was it for which I chiefly strove,
Nor stepp'd I back till I recover'd him:
I took him up and wound him in mine arms,
And welding him unto my private tent,   35
There laid him down and dew'd him with my tears,
And sigh'd and sorrow'd as became a friend.
But neither friendly sorrow, sighs nor tears,
Could win pale death from his usurped right.
Yet this I did, and less I could not do: 40
I saw him honoured with due funeral,
This scarf I pluck'd from off his lifeless arm,
And wear it in remembrance of my friend.

BEL-IMPERIA. I know the scarf, would he had kept it still,
For had he liv'd he would have kept it still,   45
And worn it for his Bel-imperia's sake:
For 'twas my favour at his last depart.
But now wear thou it both for him and me,
For after him thou hast deserv'd it best.
But for thy kindness in his life and death,   50
Be sure while Bel-imperia's life endures,
She will be Don Horatio's thankful friend.

HORATIO. And (madame) Don Horatio will not slack
Humbly to serve fair Bel-imperia.
But now if your good liking stand thereto,   55
I'll crave your pardon to go seek the Prince.
For so the Duke your father gave me charge.

     Exit.

BEL-IMPERIA. Ay, go Horatio, leave me here alone,
For solitude best fits my cheerless mood:
Yet what avails to wail Andrea's death,   60
From whence Horatio proves my second love?

Had he not loved Andrea as he did,
He could not sit in Bel-imperia's thoughts.
But how can love find harbour in my breast,
Till I revenge the death of my beloved.   65
Yes, second love shall further my revenge.
I'll love Horatio my Andrea's friend,
The more to spite the Prince that wrought his end:
And where Don Balthazar that slew my love,
Himself now pleads for favour at my hands,   70
He shall in rigour of my just disdain,
Reap long repentance for his murderous deed:
For what was 't else but murderous cowardice,
So many to oppress one valiant knight,
Without respect of honour in the fight?   75
And here he comes that murder'd my delight.

Enter LORENZO *and* BALTHAZAR.

LORENZO. Sister, what means this melancholy walk?

BEL-IMPERIA. That for a while I wish no company.

LORENZO. But here the Prince is come to visit you.

BEL-IMPERIA. That argues that he lives in liberty.   80

BALTHAZAR. No madame, but in pleasing servitude.

BEL-IMPERIA. Your prison then belike is your conceit.

BALTHAZAR. Ay by conceit my freedom is enthrall'd.

BEL-IMPERIA. Then with conceit enlarge yourself again.

BALTHAZAR. What if conceit have laid my heart to gage?   85

BEL-IMPERIA. Pay that you borrowed and recover it.

BALTHAZAR. I die if it return from whence it lies.

BEL-IMPERIA. A heartless man and live? A miracle.

BALTHAZAR. Ay lady, love can work such miracles.

LORENZO. Tush, tush my lord, let go these ambages,   90
    And in plain terms acquaint her with your love.

BEL-IMPERIA. What boots complaint, when there's no remedy?

BALTHAZAR. Yes, to your gracious self must I complain,
  In whose fair answer lies my remedy,
  On whose perfection all my thoughts attend,   95
  On whose aspect mine eyes find beauty's bower,
  In whose translucent breast my heart is lodg'd.

BEL-IMPERIA. Alas my lord these are but words of course,
  And but devise to drive me from this place.

  She in going in, lets fall her glove, which HORATIO *coming
  out takes up.*

HORATIO. Madame, your glove.   100

BEL-IMPERIA. Thanks good Horatio, take it for thy pains.

BALTHAZAR. Signior Horatio stoop'd in happy time.

HORATIO. I reap'd more grace than I deserv'd or hop'd.

LORENZO. My lord, be not dismay'd for what is past,
  You know that women oft are humorous: 105
  These clouds will overblow with little wind.
  Let me alone, I'll scatter them myself:
  Meanwhile let us devise to spend the time,
  In some delightful sports and revelling.

HORATIO. The King my lords is coming hither straight,   110
  To feast the Portingale ambassador,
  Things were in readiness before I came.

BALTHAZAR. Then here it fits us to attend the King,
  To welcome hither our ambassador,
  And learn my father and my country's health.   115

  Enter the banquet, trumpets, the KING *and* AMBASSADOR.

KING. See Lord Ambassador, how Spain entreats
  Their prisoner Balthazar, thy Viceroy's son:
  We pleasure more in kindness than in wars.

AMBASSADOR. Sad is our King, and Portingale laments,
  Supposing that Don Balthazar is slain.   120

BALTHAZAR. So am I slain by beauty's tyranny. [*Aside.*]
    You see my lord how Balthazar is slain.
    I frolic with the Duke of Castile's son,
    Wrapp'd every hour in pleasures of the Court,
    And grac'd with favours of his majesty.   125

KING. Put off your greetings till our feast be done,
    Now come and sit with us and taste our cheer.

Sit to the banquet.

    Sit down young Prince, you are our second guest:
    Brother sit down, and nephew take your place,
    Signior Horatio wait thou upon our cup,   130
    For well thou hast deserved to be honour'd.
    Now lordings fall to, Spain is Portugal,
    And Portugal is Spain, we both are friends,
    Tribute is paid, and we enjoy our right.
    But where is old Hieronimo, our Marshal,   135
    He promis'd us in honour of our guest,
    To grace our banquet with some pompous jest.

Enter HIERONIMO *with a drum, three* KNIGHTS, *each his*
scutcheon, then he fetches THREE KINGS, *they* [*the* KNIGHTS] *take*
their crowns and them captive.

    Hieronimo, this masque contents mine eye,
    Although I sound not well the mystery.   139

HIERONIMO. The first arm'd knight, that hung his scutcheon up,

He takes the scutcheon and gives it to the KING.

    Was English Robert Earl of Gloucester,
    Who when King Stephen bore sway in Albion,
    Arriv'd with five and twenty thousand men,
    In Portingale, and by success of war,
    Enforc'd the King, then but a Saracen,   145
    To bear the yoke of the English monarchy.

KING. My lord of Portingale, by this you see,
    That which may comfort both your King and you,
    And make your late discomfort seem the less.
    But say Hieronimo, what was the next?   150

HIERONIMO. The second knight that hung his scutcheon up,

He doth as he did before.

Was Edmund Earl of Kent in Albion,
When English Richard wore the diadem.
He came likewise and razed Lisbon walls,
And took the King of Portingale in fight: 155
For which, and other such like service done,
He after was created Duke of York.

KING. This is another special argument,
That Portingale may deign to bear our yoke,
When it by little England hath been yok'd: 160
But now Hieronimo what were the last?

HIERONIMO. The third and last not least in our account,

Doing as before.

Was as the rest a valiant Englishman,
Brave John of Gaunt the Duke of Lancaster,
As by his scutcheon plainly may appear.   165
He with a puissant army came to Spain,
And took our King of Castile prisoner.

AMBASSADOR. This is an argument for our Viceroy,
That Spain may not insult for her success,
Since English warriors likewise conquer'd Spain,   170
And made them bow their knees to Albion.

KING. Hieronimo, I drink to thee for this device,
Which hath pleas'd both the ambassador and me:
Pledge me Hieronimo, if thou love the King.

Takes the cup of HORATIO.

My lord, I fear we sit but over-long   175
Unless our dainties were more delicate.
But welcome are you to the best we have.
Now let us in that you may be despatch'd,
I think our council is already set.

Exeunt omnes.

Act I, Scene v

GHOST. Come we for this from depth of under ground,
    To see him feast that gave me my death's wound?
    These pleasant sights are sorrow to my soul,
    Nothing but league, and love and banqueting?

REVENGE. Be still Andrea ere we go from hence,   5
    I'll turn their friendship into fell despite,
    Their love to mortal hate, their day to night,
    Their hope into despair, their peace to war,
    Their joys to pain, their bliss to misery.

Act II, Scene i

Enter LORENZO *and* BALTHAZAR.

LORENZO. My lord, though Bel-imperia seem thus coy,
    Let reason hold you in your wonted joy:
    In time the savage bull sustains the yoke,
    In time all haggard hawks will stoop to lure,
    In time small wedges cleave the hardest oak,   5
    In time the flint is pierc'd with softest shower,
    And she in time will fall from her disdain,
    And rue the sufferance of your friendly pain.

BALTHAZAR. No, she is wilder, and more hard withal,
    Than beast, or bird, or tree, or stony wall.   10
    But wherefore blot I Bel-imperia's name?
    It is my fault, not she that merits blame.
    My feature is not to content her sight,
    My words are rude and work her no delight.
    The lines I send her are but harsh and ill,   15
    Such as do drop from Pan and Marsyas' quill.
    My presents are not of sufficient cost,
    And being worthless all my labour's lost.
    Yet might she love me for my valiancy,
    Ay, but that's sland'red by captivity.   20
    Yet might she love me to content her sire:
    Ay, but her reason masters his desire.
    Yet might she love me as her brother's friend,
    Ay, but her hopes aim at some other end.
    Yet might she love me to uprear her state,   25
    Ay, but perhaps she hopes some nobler mate.
    Yet might she love me as her beauty's thrall,
    Ay, but I fear she cannot love at all.

LORENZO. My lord, for my sake leave these ecstasies,

And doubt not but we'll find some remedy,   30
Some cause there is that lets you not be lov'd:
First that must needs be known and then remov'd.
What if my sister love some other knight?

BALTHAZAR. My summer's day will turn to winter's night.

LORENZO. I have already found a stratagem,   35
To sound the bottom of this doubtful theme.
My lord, for once you shall be rul'd by me,
Hinder me not whate'er you hear or see.
By force or fair means will I cast about,
To find the truth of all this question out.   40
Ho Pedringano!

PEDRINGANO. Signior.

LORENZO.   *Vien qui presto.*

Enter PEDRINGANO.

PEDRINGANO. Hath your lordship any service to command me?

LORENZO. Ay, Pedringano service of import,
And not to spend the time in trifling words,
Thus stands the case: it is not long thou know'st,   45
Since I did shield thee from my father's wrath,
For thy conveyance in Andrea's love:
For which thou wert adjudg'd to punishment,
I stood betwixt thee and thy punishment:
And since, thou know'st how I have favour'd thee.   50
Now to these favours will I add reward,
Not with fair words, but store of golden coin,
And lands and living join'd with dignities,
If thou but satisfy my just demand.
Tell truth and have me for thy lasting friend.   55

PEDRINGANO. Whate'er it be your lordship shall demand,
My bounden duty bids me tell the truth,
If case it lie in me to tell the truth

LORENZO. Then Pedringano this is my demand,
Whom loves my sister Bel-imperia?   60

For she reposeth all her trust in thee:
Speak man and gain both friendship and reward,
I mean, whom loves she in Andrea's place?

PEDRINGANO. Alas my lord, since Don Andrea's death,
I have no credit with her as before,   65
And therefore know not if she love or no.

LORENZO. Nay if thou dally then I am thy foe,
And fear shall force what friendship cannot win.
Thy death shall bury what thy life conceals.
Thou diest for more esteeming her than me.   70

PEDRINGANO. O stay my lord.

LORENZO. Yet speak the truth and I will guerdon thee,
And shield thee from whatever can ensue.
And will conceal whate'er proceeds from thee,
But if thou dally once again, thou diest.   75

PEDRINGANO. If Madame Bel-imperia be in love –

LORENZO. What villain, ifs and ands?

PEDRINGANO. O stay my lord, she loves Horatio.

BALTHAZAR *starts back.*

LORENZO. What Don Horatio our Knight Marshal's son?

PEDRINGANO. Even him my lord.   80

LORENZO. Now say, but how know'st thou he is her love,
And thou shalt find me kind and liberal:
Stand up I say, and fearless tell the truth.

PEDRINGANO. She sent him letters which myself perus'd,
Full fraught with lines and arguments of love,   85
Preferring him before Prince Balthazar.

LORENZO. Swear on this cross, that what thou say'st is true,
And that thou wilt conceal what thou hast told.

PEDRINGANO. I swear to both by him that made us all.

LORENZO. In hope thine oath is true, here's thy reward,   90

But if I prove thee perjur'd and unjust,
This very sword whereon thou took'st thine oath,
Shall be the worker of thy tragedy.

PEDRINGANO. What I have said is true, and shall for me,
  Be still conceal'd from Bel-imperia.   95
  Besides your honour's liberality
  Deserves my duteous service, even till death.

LORENZO. Let this be all that thou shalt do for me,
  Be watchful when, and where these lovers meet,
  And give me notice in some secret sort.   100

PEDRINGANO. I will my lord.

LORENZO. Then shalt thou find that I am liberal,
  Thou know'st that I can more advance thy state
  Than she, be therefore wise and fail me not.
  Go and attend her as thy custom is,   105
  Lest absence make her think thou dost amiss.

  Exit PEDRINGANO.

  Why so: *tam armis quam ingenio.*
  Where words prevail not, violence prevails.
  But gold doth more than either of them both.
  How likes Prince Balthazar this stratagem?   110

BALTHAZAR. Both well, and ill: it makes me glad and sad:
  Glad, that I know the hinderer of my love,
  Sad, that I fear she hates me whom I love.
  Glad, that I know on whom to be reveng'd,
  Sad, that she'll fly me if I take revenge.   115
  Yet must I take revenge or die myself,
  For love resisted grows impatient.
  I think Horatio be my destin'd plague,
  First in his hand he brandished a sword,
  And with that sword he fiercely waged war,   120
  And in that war he gave me dangerous wounds,
  And by those wounds he forced me to yield,
  And by my yielding I became his slave.
  Now in his mouth he carries pleasing words,

Which pleasing words do harbour sweet conceits,   125
Which sweet conceits are lim'd with sly deceits,
Which sly deceits smooth Bel-imperia's ears,
And through her ears dive down into her heart,
And in her heart set him where I should stand.
Thus hath he ta'en my body by his force,   130
And now by sleight would captivate my soul:
But in his fall I'll tempt the destinies,
And either lose my life, or win my love.

LORENZO. Let's go my lord, your staying stays revenge.
Do you but follow me and gain your love,   135
Her favour must be won by his remove.

Exeunt.

Act II, Scene ii

Enter HORATIO *and* BEL-IMPERIA.

HORATIO. Now madame, since by favour of your love,
Our hidden smoke is turn'd to open flame:
And that with looks and words we feed our thoughts,
Two chief contents, where more cannot be had.
Thus in the midst of love's fair blandishments,   5
Why show you sign of inward languishments.

PEDRINGANO *showeth all to the* PRINCE *and* LORENZO,
placing them in secret.

BEL-IMPERIA. My heart (sweet friend) is like a ship at sea,
She wisheth port, where riding all at ease,
She may repair what stormy times have worn:
And leaning on the shore may sing with joy,   10
That pleasure follows pain, and bliss annoy.
Possession of thy love is th' only port,
Wherein my heart with fears and hopes long toss'd,
Each hour doth wish and long to make resort,
There to repair the joys that it hath lost: 15

And sitting safe to sing in Cupid's choir,
That sweetest bliss is crown of love's desire.

BALTHAZAR *above.*

BALTHAZAR. O sleep mine eyes, see not my love profan'd,
  Be deaf my ears, hear not my discontent,
  Die heart, another joys what thou deservest.   20

LORENZO. Watch still mine eyes, to see this love disjoin'd,
  Hear still mine ears, to hear them both lament,
  Live heart to joy at fond Horatio's fall.

BEL-IMPERIA. Why stands Horatio speechless all this while?

HORATIO. The less I speak, the more I meditate.   25

BEL-IMPERIA. But whereon dost thou chiefly meditate?

HORATIO. On dangers past, and pleasures to ensue.

BALTHAZAR. On pleasures past, and dangers to ensue.

BEL-IMPERIA. What dangers, and what pleasures dost thou mean?

HORATIO. Dangers of war, and pleasures of our love.   30

LORENZO. Dangers of death, but pleasures none at all.

BEL-IMPERIA. Let dangers go, thy war shall be with me,
  But such a warring, as breaks no bond of peace.
  Speak thou fair words, I'll cross them with fair words,
  Send thou sweet looks, I'll meet them with sweet looks,   35
  Write loving lines, I'll answer loving lines,
  Give me a kiss, I'll countercheck thy kiss,
  Be this our warring peace, or peaceful war.

HORATIO. But gracious madame, then appoint the field,
  Where trial of this war shall first be made.   40

BALTHAZAR. Ambitious villain, how his boldness grows?

BEL-IMPERIA. Then be thy father's pleasant bower the field,
  Where first we vow'd a mutual amity:
  The court were dangerous, that place is safe:
  Our hour shall be when Vesper 'gins to rise,   45

That summons home distressful travellers.
There none shall hear us but the harmless birds,
Happily the gentle nightingale,
Shall carol us asleep ere we be ware,
And singing with the prickle at her breast,   50
Tell our delight and mirthful dalliance.
Till then each hour will seem a year and more.

HORATIO. But honey sweet, and honourable love,
    Return we now into your father's sight,
    Dangerous suspicion waits on our delight.   55

LORENZO. Ay, danger mixed with jealous despite,
    Shall send thy soul into eternal night.

Exeunt.

Act II, Scene iii

Enter KING *of Spain, Portingale* AMBASSADOR, [*Don Cyprian, Duke of*] CASTILE, *etc.*

KING. Brother of Castile, to the Prince's love:
    What says your daughter Bel-imperia?

CASTILE. Although she coy it as becomes her kind,
    And yet dissemble that she loves the Prince:
    I doubt not I, but she will stoop in time.   5
    And were she froward, which she will not be,
    Yet herein shall she follow my advice,
    Which is to love him or forgo my love.
KING. Then Lord Ambassador of Portingale,
    Advise thy King to make this marriage up,   10
    For strengthening of our late confirmed league,
    I know no better means to make us friends.
    Her dowry shall be large and liberal,
    Besides that, she is daughter and half heir,
    Unto our brother here Don Cyprian,   15
    And shall enjoy the moiety of his land.

I'll grace her marriage with an uncle's gift,
And this it is, in case the match go forward,
The tribute which you pay shall be releas'd,
And if by Balthazar she have a son,   20
He shall enjoy the kingdom after us.

AMBASSADOR. I'll make the motion to my sovereign liege,
And work it if my counsel may prevail.

KING. Do so my lord, and if he give consent,
I hope his presence here will honour us,   25
In celebration of the nuptial day,
And let himself determine of the time.

AMBASSADOR. Will 't please your grace command me aught
beside?

KING. Commend me to the King, and so farewell.
But where's Prince Balthazar to take his leave?   30

AMBASSADOR. That is perform'd already, my good lord.

KING. Amongst the rest of what you have in charge,
The Prince's ransom must not be forgot:
That's none of mine, but his that took him prisoner,
And well his forwardness deserves reward.   35
It was Horatio our Knight Marshal's son.

AMBASSADOR. Between us there's a price already pitch'd,
And shall be sent with all convenient speed.

KING. Then once again farewell my lord.

AMBASSADOR. Farewell my Lord of Castile and the rest.   40

Exit.

KING. Now brother, you must take some little pains,
To win fair Bel-imperia from her will:
Young virgins must be ruled by their friends,
The Prince is amiable and loves her well,
If she neglect him and forgo his love,   45
She both will wrong her own estate and ours:
Therefore whiles I do entertain the Prince,

With greatest pleasure that our Court affords,
Endeavour you to win your daughter's thought,
If she give back, all this will come to naught.   50

Exeunt.

Act II, Scene iv

Enter HORATIO, BEL-IMPERIA, *and* PEDRINGANO.

HORATIO. Now that the night begins with sable wings,
    To over-cloud the brightness of the sun,
    And that in darkness pleasures may be done:
    Come Bel-imperia let us to the bower,
    And there in safety pass a pleasant hour.   5

BEL-IMPERIA. I follow thee my love, and will not back,
    Although my fainting heart controls my soul.

HORATIO. Why, make you doubt of Pedringano's faith?

BEL-IMPERIA. No he is trusty as my second self.
    Go Pedringano watch without the gate,   10
    And let us know if any make approach.

PEDRINGANO. Instead of watching, I'll deserve more gold,
    By fetching Don Lorenzo to this match. [*Aside.*]

    Exit PEDRINGANO.

HORATIO. What means my love?

BEL-IMPERIA.   I know not what myself:
    And yet my heart foretells me some mischance.   15

HORATIO. Sweet say not so, fair fortune is our friend,
    And heavens have shut up day to pleasure us.
    The stars thou see'st hold back their twinkling shine,
    And Luna hides her self to pleasure us.   19

BEL-IMPERIA. Thou hast prevail'd, I'll conquer my misdoubt,
    And in thy love and counsel drown my fear:

I fear no more, love now is all my thoughts.
Why sit we not, for pleasure asketh ease?

HORATIO. The more thou sit'st within these leafy bowers,
The more will Flora deck it with her flowers.   25

BEL-IMPERIA. Ay but if Flora spy Horatio here,
Her jealous eye will think I sit too near.

HORATIO. Hark madame how the birds record by night,
For joy that Bel-imperia sits in sight.

BEL-IMPERIA. No, Cupid counterfeits the nightingale,   30
To frame sweet music to Horatio's tale.

HORATIO. If Cupid sing, then Venus is not far,
Ay, thou art Venus or some fairer star.

BEL-IMPERIA. If I be Venus, thou must needs be Mars,
And where Mars reigneth there must needs be wars.   35

HORATIO. Then thus begin our wars: put forth thy hand,
That it may combat with my ruder hand.

BEL-IMPERIA. Set forth thy foot to try the push of mine.

HORATIO. But first my looks shall combat against thine.

BEL-IMPERIA. Then ward thyself, I dart this kiss at thee.   40

HORATIO. Thus I retort the dart thou threw'st at me.

BEL-IMPERIA. Nay then to gain the glory of the field,
My twining arms shall yoke and make thee yield.

HORATIO. Nay then my arms are large and strong withal:
Thus elms by vines are compass'd till they fall.   45

BEL-IMPERIA. O let me go, for in my troubled eyes,
Now may'st thou read that life in passion dies.

HORATIO. O stay a while and I will die with thee,
So shalt thou yield, and yet have conquer'd me.

BEL-IMPERIA. Who's there Pedringano? We are betray'd.   50

Enter LORENZO, BALTHAZAR, SERBERINE,
PEDRINGANO, *disguised.*

LORENZO. My lord away with her, take her aside.
  O sir forbear, your valour is already tried.
  Quickly despatch, my masters.

They hang him in the arbour.

HORATIO. What, will you murder me?

LORENZO. Ay thus, and thus, these are the fruits of love.   55

They stab him.

BEL-IMPERIA. O save his life and let me die for him.
  O save him brother, save him Balthazar:
  I lov'd Horatio but he lov'd not me.

BALTHAZAR. But Balthazar loves Bel-imperia.

LORENZO. Although his life were still ambitious proud,   60
  Yet is he at the highest now he is dead.

BEL-IMPERIA. Murder, murder, help Hieronimo, help.

LORENZO. Come stop her mouth, away with her.

Exeunt.

Enter HIERONIMO *in his shirt, etc.*

HIERONIMO. What outcries pluck me from my naked bed,
  And chill my throbbing heart with trembling fear,   65
  Which never danger yet could daunt before.
  Who calls Hieronimo? Speak, here I am:
  I did not slumber, therefore 'twas no dream,
  No, no, it was some woman cried for help,
  And here within this garden did she cry.   70
  And in this garden must I rescue her:
  But stay, what murd'rous spectacle is this?
  A man hang'd up and all the murderers gone,
  And in my bower to lay the guilt on me:
  This place was made for pleasure not for death.   75

He cuts him down.

  Those garments that he wears I oft have seen,
  Alas it is Horatio my sweet son.
  Oh no, but he that whilom was my son,

O was it thou that call'dst me from my bed,
O speak if any spark of life remain.   80
I am thy father, who hath slain my son?
What savage monster, not of human kind,
Hath here been glutted with thy harmless blood?
And left thy bloody corpse dishonoured here,
For me amidst this dark and deathful shades,   85
To drown thee with an ocean of my tears.
O heavens, why made you night to cover sin?
By day this deed of darkness had not been.
O earth why didst thou not in time devour,
The vild profaner of this sacred bower.   90
O poor Horatio, what hadst thou misdone?
To leese thy life ere life was new begun.
O wicked butcher whatsoe'er thou wert,
How could thou strangle virtue and desert?
Ay me most wretched, that have lost my joy,   95
In leesing my Horatio my sweet boy.

Enter ISABELLA.

ISABELLA. My husband's absence makes my heart to throb:
    Hieronimo!

HIERONIMO. Here Isabella, help me to lament,
    For sighs are stopp'd and all my tears are spent.   100

ISABELLA. What world of grief, my son Horatio?
    O where's the author of this endless woe.

HIERONIMO. To know the author were some ease of grief,
    For in revenge my heart would find relief.

ISABELLA. Then is he gone? And is my son gone too?   105
    O, gush out tears, fountains and floods of tears,
    Blow sighs and raise an everlasting storm.
    For outrage fits our cursed wretchedness.

HIERONIMO. Sweet lovely rose, ill pluck'd before thy time,
    Fair worthy son, not conquered, but betray'd: 110
    I'll kiss thee now, for words with tears are stay'd.

ISABELLA. And I'll close up the glasses of his sight,
    For once these eyes were only my delight.

HIERONIMO. See'st thou this handkercher besmear'd with blood,
    It shall not from me till I take revenge: 115
    See'st thou those wounds that yet are bleeding fresh,
    I'll not entomb them till I have reveng'd:
    Then will I joy amidst my discontent,
    Till then my sorrow never shall be spent.

ISABELLA. The heavens are just, murder cannot be hid,   120
    Time is the author both of truth and right,
    And time will bring this treachery to light.

HIERONIMO. Meanwhile good Isabella cease thy plaints,
    Or at the least dissemble them a while,
    So shall we sooner find the practice out,   125
    And learn by whom all this was brought about.
    Come Isabel now let us take him up.

They take him up.

    And bear him in from out this cursed place.
    I'll say his dirge, singing fits not this case.
    O aliquis mihi quas pulchrum var educat herbas,   130

HIERONIMO *sets his breast unto his sword.*

Misceat et nostro detur, medicina dolori:
Aut si qui faciunt animis oblimia succos,
Prebeat, ipse metum magnam quicunque per orbem,
Gramina Sol pulchras effecit in luminis oras.
Ipse bibam quicquid meditatur saga veneri.   135
Quicquid et irravi eve caeca menia nectit.
Omnia perpetiar, lethum quoque dum semel omnis,
Noster in extincto moriatur pectora sensus:
Ergo tuos occulos nunquam (mea vita) videbo.
Et tua perpetuus sepelivit lumina somnus: 140
Emoriar tecum sic, sic juvat ire sub umbras,
Attamen absistam properato cedere letho,
Ne mortem vindicta tuam tam nulla sequatur.

Here he throws it from him and bears the body away.

Act II, Scene v

GHOST. Brought'st thou me hither to increase my pain?
　　I look'd that Balthazar should have been slain:
　　But 'tis my friend Horatio that is slain,
　　And they abuse fair Bel-imperia,
　　On whom I doted more than all the world,
　　Because she lov'd me more than all the world.　　　5

REVENGE. Thou talk'st of harvest when the corn is green,
　　The end is crown of every work well done:
　　The sickle comes not till the corn be ripe.
　　Be still, and ere I lead thee from this place,　　　10
　　I'll show thee Balthazar in heavy case.

Act III, Scene i

Enter VICEROY *of Portingale,* NOBLES, VILLUPPO.

VICEROY. Infortunate condition of kings,
    Seated amidst so many helpless doubts.
    First we are plac'd upon extremest height,
    And oft supplanted with exceeding heat,
    But ever subject to the wheel of chance: 5
    And at our highest never joy we so,
    As we both doubt and dread our overthrow.
    So striveth not the waves with sundry winds,
    As Fortune toileth in the affairs of kings,
    That would be fear'd, yet fear to be belov'd,   10
    Sith fear or love to kings is flattery.
    For instance lordings, look upon your King,
    By hate deprived of his dearest son,
    The only hope of our successive line.

FIRST NOBLE. I had not thought that Alexandro's heart   15
    Had been envenom'd with such extreme hate:
    But now I see that words have several works,
    And there's no credit in the countenance.

VILLUPPO. No, for, my lord, had you beheld the train,
    That feigned love had coloured in his looks,   20
    When he in camp consorted Balthazar:
    Far more inconstant had you thought the sun,
    That hourly coasts the centre of the earth,
    Than Alexandro's purpose to the Prince.

VICEROY. No more Villuppo, thou hast said enough,   25
    And with thy words thou slay'st our wounded thoughts.
    Nor shall I longer dally with the world,
    Procrastinating Alexandro's death:

Go some of you and fetch the traitor forth,
That as he is condemned he may die.   30

Enter ALEXANDRO *with a* NOBLEMAN *and* HALBERTS.

SECOND NOBLE. In such extremes, will naught but patience
    serve.

ALEXANDRO. But in extremes, what patience shall I use?
    Nor discontents it me to leave the world,
    With whom there nothing can prevail but wrong.   34

SECOND NOBLE. Yet hope the best.

ALEXANDRO.   'Tis Heaven is my hope.
    As for the earth it is too much infect,
    To yield me hope of any of her mould.

VICEROY. Why linger ye? Bring forth that daring fiend,
    And let him die for his accursed deed.

ALEXANDRO. Not that I fear the extremity of death,   40
    For nobles cannot stoop to servile fear,
    Do I (O King) thus discontented live.
    But this, O this torments my labouring soul,
    That thus I die suspected of a sin,
    Whereof, as heavens have known my secret thoughts,   45
    So am I free from this suggestion.

VICEROY. No more I say, to the tortures, when?
    Bind him, and burn his body in those flames,

They bind him to the stake.

    That shall prefigure those unquenched fires,
    Of Phlegethon prepared for his soul.   50

ALEXANDRO. My guiltless death will be aveng'd on thee,
    On thee Villuppo that hath malic'd thus,
    Or for thy meed, hast falsely me accus'd.

VILLUPPO. Nay Alexandro if thou menace me,
    I'll lend a hand to send thee to the lake,   55

Where those thy words shall perish with thy works,
Injurious traitor, monstrous homicide.

Enter AMBASSADOR.

AMBASSADOR. Stay hold a while,
And here with pardon of his majesty,
Lay hands upon Villuppo.

VICEROY.   Ambassador,   60
What news hath urg'd this sudden entrance?

AMBASSADOR. Know sovereign lord that Balthazar doth live.

VICEROY. What say'st thou? Liveth Balthazar our son?

AMBASSADOR. Your highness' son, Lord Balthazar, doth live,
And well entreated in the Court of Spain: 65
Humbly commends him to your majesty.
These eyes beheld, and these my followers,
With these the letters of the King's commends,

Gives him letters.

Are happy witnesses of his highness' health.

The [VICEROY] *looks on the letters, and proceeds.*

VICEROY. 'Thy son doth live, your tribute is receiv'd,   70
Thy peace is made, and we are satisfied:
The rest resolve upon as things propos'd,
For both our honours and thy benefit.'

AMBASSADOR. These are his highness' farther articles.

He gives him more letters.

VICEROY. Accursed wretch to intimate these ills,   75
Against the life and reputation
Of noble Alexandro. Come my lord unbind him.
Let him unbind thee that is bound to death,
To make a quital for thy discontent.   79

They unbind him.

ALEXANDRO. Dread lord, in kindness you could do no less,
    Upon report of such a damned fact:
    But thus we see our innocence hath sav'd,
    The hopeless life which thou Villuppo sought,
    By thy suggestions to have massacred.

VICEROY. Say false Villuppo, wherefore didst thou thus 85
    Falsely betray Lord Alexandro's life?
    Him whom thou knowest, that no unkindness else,
    But even the slaughter of our dearest son,
    Could once have mov'd us to have misconceiv'd.

ALEXANDRO. Say treacherous Villuppo, tell the King,   90
    Or wherein hath Alexandro us'd thee ill?

VILLUPPO. Rent with remembrance of so foul a deed,
    My guilty soul submits me to thy doom:
    For not for Alexandro's injuries,
    But, for reward, and hope to be preferr'd,   95
    Thus have I shamelessly hazarded his life.

VICEROY. Which villain shall be ransom'd with thy death,
    And not so mean a torment as we here
    Devis'd for him, who thou said'st slew our son:
    But with the bitterest torments and extremes,   100
    That may be yet invented for thine end.

    ALEXANDRO *seems to entreat.*

    Entreat me not, go take the traitor hence.

    Exit VILLUPPO.

    And Alexandro let us honour thee,
    With public notice of thy loyalty,
    To end those things articulated here,   105
    By our great lord the mighty King of Spain.
    We with our council will deliberate,
    Come Alexandro keep us company.

    Exeunt.

Act III, Scene ii

Enter HIERONIMO.

HIERONIMO. O eyes, no eyes but fountains fraught with tears,
  O life, no life, but lively form of death:
  O world, no world but mass of public wrongs,
  Confus'd and fill'd, with murder and misdeeds.
  O sacred heavens, if this unhallowed deed,   5
  If this inhumane and barbarous attempt,
  If this incomparable murder thus,
  Of mine, but now no more my son,
  Shall unreveal'd and unrevenged pass,
  How should we term your dealings to be just,   10
  If you unjustly deal with those, that in your justice trust.
  The night, sad secretary to my moans,
  With direful visions wake my vexed soul,
  And with the wounds of my distressful son,
  Solicit me for notice of his death.   15
  The ugly fiends do sally forth of hell,
  And frame my steps to unfrequented paths,
  And fear my heart with fierce inflamed thoughts.
  The cloudy day my discontents records,
  Early begins to register my dreams,   20
  And drive me forth to seek the murderer.
  Eyes, life, world, heavens, hell, night and day,
  See, search, show, send some man, some mean, that may –

A letter falleth.

What's here? A letter, tush, it is not so,
A letter written to Hieronimo.   25

Red ink.

'For want of ink, receive this bloody writ,
Me hath my hapless brother hid from thee,
Revenge thyself on Balthazar and him,
For these were they that murdered thy son.
Hieronimo, revenge Horatio's death,   30
And better fare than Bel-imperia doth.'

What means this unexpected miracle?
My son slain by Lorenzo and the Prince.
What cause had they Horatio to malign?
Or what might move thee Bel-imperia, 35
To accuse thy brother, had he been the mean?
Hieronimo, beware, thou art betray'd,
And to entrap thy life this train is laid.
Advise thee therefore, be not credulous:
This is devised to endanger thee, 40
That thou by this Lorenzo should'st accuse,
And he for thy dishonour done, should draw
Thy life in question, and thy name in hate.
Dear was the life of my beloved son,
And of his death behoves me be reveng'd: 45
Then hazard not thine own Hieronimo,
But live t' effect thy resolution.
I therefore will by circumstances try,
What I can gather to confirm this writ,
And, hearkening near the Duke of Castile's house, 50
Close if I can with Bel-imperia,
To listen more, but nothing to bewray.

Enter PEDRINGANO.

Now Pedringano.

PEDRINGANO.   Now Hieronimo.

HIERONIMO. Where's thy lady?

PEDRINGANO.   I know not, here's my lord.

Enter LORENZO.

LORENZO. How now, who's this, Hieronimo?

HIERONIMO.   My lord. 55

PEDRINGANO. He asketh for my lady Bel-imperia.

LORENZO. What to do Hieronimo? The Duke my father hath
    Upon some disgrace a while remov'd her hence,
    But if it be aught I may inform her of,
    Tell me Hieronimo, and I'll let her know it. 60

HIERONIMO. Nay, nay my lord, I thank you, it shall not need,
  I had a suit unto her, but too late,
  And her disgrace makes me unfortunate.

LORENZO. Why so, Hieronimo? Use me.

HIERONIMO. O no my lord, I dare not, it must not be.   65
  I humbly thank your lordship.

LORENZO.   Why then farewell.

HIERONIMO. My grief no heart, my thoughts no tongue can tell.

  Exit.

LORENZO. Come hither Pedringano, see'st thou this?

PEDRINGANO. My lord, I see it, and suspect it too.

LORENZO. This is that damned villain Serberine,   70
  That hath I fear reveal'd Horatio's death.

PEDRINGANO. My lord, he could not, 'twas so lately done,
  And since he hath not left my company.

LORENZO. Admit he have not, his condition's such,
  As fear or flattering words may make him false,   75
  I know his humour, and therewith repent,
  That e'er I used him in this enterprise.
  But Pedringano, to prevent the worst,
  And 'cause I know thee secret as my soul,
  Here for thy further satisfaction take thou this,   80

  Gives him more gold.

  And hearken to me, thus it is devis'd:
  This night thou must, and prithee so resolve,
  Meet Serberine at Saint Luigi's Park,
  Thou know'st 'tis here hard by behind the house,
  There take thy stand, and see thou strike him sure,   85
  For die he must, if we do mean to live.

PEDRINGANO. But how shall Serberine be there my lord?

LORENZO. Let me alone, I'll send to him to meet
   The Prince and me, where thou must do this deed.

PEDRINGANO. It shall be done my lord, it shall be done,   90
   And I'll go arm myself to meet him there.

LORENZO. When things shall alter, as I hope they will,
   Then shalt thou mount for this, thou know'st my mind.

Exit PEDRINGANO.

Che le Ieron.

Enter PAGE.

PAGE.   My lord?

LORENZO.   Go sirrah to Serberine,
   And bid him forthwith meet the Prince and me   95
   At Saint Luigi's Park, behind the house,
   This evening, boy.

PAGE.   I go my lord.

LORENZO. But sirrah, let the hour be eight o'clock.
   Bid him not fail.

PAGE.   I fly, my lord.

Exit.

LORENZO. Now to confirm the complot thou hast cast   100
   Of all these practices, I'll spread the watch,
   Upon precise commandment from the King,
   Strongly to guard the place where Pedringano
   This night shall murder hapless Serberine.
   Thus must we work that will avoid distrust,   105
   Thus must we practise to prevent mishap,
   And thus one ill, another must expulse.
   This sly enquiry of Hieronimo
   For Bel-imperia, breeds suspicion,
   And this suspicion bodes a further ill.   110
   As for myself, I know my secret fault,
   And so do they, but I have dealt for them.

They that for coin their souls endangered
To save my life, for coin shall venture theirs:
And better 'tis that base companions die,   115
Than by their life to hazard our good haps.
Nor shall they live for me, to fear their faith:
I'll trust myself, myself shall be my friend,
For die they shall, slaves are ordained to no other end.

Exit.

Act III, Scene iii

Enter PEDRINGANO *with a pistol.*

PEDRINGANO. Now Pedringano bid thy pistol hold,
    And hold on Fortune, once more favour me,
    Give but success to mine attempting spirit,
    And let me shift for taking of mine aim:
    Here is the gold, this is the gold propos'd,   5
    It is no dream that I adventure for,
    But Pedringano is possess'd thereof.
    And he that would not strain his conscience,
    For him that thus his liberal purse hath stretch'd,
    Unworthy such a favour may he fail,   10
    And wishing, want when such as I prevail.
    As for the fear of apprehension,
    I know, if need should be, my noble lord
    Will stand between me and ensuing harms.
    Besides, this place is free from all suspect: 15
    Here therefore will I stay and take my stand.

    Enter the WATCH.

FIRST WATCH. I wonder much to what intent it is,
    That we are thus expressly charg'd to watch?

SECOND WATCH. 'Tis by commandment in the King's
        own name.

THIRD WATCH. But we were never wont to watch and ward,
    So near the Duke his brother's house before.   21

SECOND WATCH. Content yourself, stand close, there's
      somewhat in 't.

Enter SERBERINE.

SERBERINE. Here Serberine attend and stay thy pace,
    For here did Don Lorenzo's page appoint,
    That thou by his command shouldst meet with him.   25
    How fit a place if one were so dispos'd,
    Methinks this corner is to close with one.

PEDRINGANO. Here comes the bird that I must seize upon,
    Now Pedringano or never play the man.

SERBERINE. I wonder that his lordship stays so long,   30
    Or wherefore should he send for me so late?

PEDRINGANO. For this Serberine, and thou shalt ha 't.

    Shoots the dag

    So, there he lies, my promise is perform'd.

    The WATCH [*approach*].

FIRST WATCH. Hark gentlemen, this is a pistol shot.

SECOND WATCH. And here's one slain, stay the murderer.   35

PEDRINGANO. Now by the sorrows of the souls in hell,

    He strives with the WATCH.

    Who first lays hand on me, I'll be his priest.

THIRD WATCH. Sirrah, confess, and therein play the priest,
    Why hast thou thus unkindly kill'd the man?

PEDRINGANO. Why, because he walk'd abroad so late.   40

THIRD WATCH. Come sir, you had been better kept your bed,
    Than have committed this misdeed so late.

SECOND WATCH. Come to the Marshal's with the murderer.

FIRST WATCH. On to Hieronimo's, help me here,
    To bring the murd'red body with us too.   45

PEDRINGANO. Hieronimo, carry me before whom you will,
    Whate'er he be I'll answer him and you.
    And do your worst, for I defy you all.

    Exeunt.

Act III, Scene iv

Enter LORENZO *and* BALTHAZAR.

BALTHAZAR. How now my lord, what makes you rise so soon?

LORENZO. Fear of preventing our mishaps too late.

BALTHAZAR. What mischief is it that we not mistrust?

LORENZO. Our greatest ills, we least mistrust my lord,
    And inexpected harms do hurt us most.   5

BALTHAZAR. Why tell me Don Lorenzo, tell me man,
    If aught concerns our honour and your own?

LORENZO. Nor you nor me my lord, but both in one.
    For I suspect, and the presumption's great,
    That by those base confederates in our fault,   10
    Touching the death of Don Horatio:
    We are betray'd to old Hieronimo.

BALTHAZAR. Betray'd, Lorenzo, tush it cannot be.

LORENZO. A guilty conscience urged with the thought
    Of former evils, easily cannot err: 15
    I am persuaded, and dissuade me not,
    That all's revealed to Hieronimo.
    And therefore know that I have cast it thus –

    [*Enter* PAGE.]

    But here's the page, how now, what news with thee?

PAGE. My lord, Serberine is slain.   20

BALTHAZAR. Who? Serberine my man.

PAGE. Your highness' man, my lord.

LORENZO. Speak page, who murdered him?

PAGE. He that is apprehended for the fact.

LORENZO. Who?   25

PAGE. Pedringano.

BALTHAZAR Is Serberine slain that lov'd his lord so well?
    Injurious villain, murderer of his friend.

LORENZO. Hath Pedringano murdered Serberine?
    My lord, let me entreat you to take the pains   30
    To exasperate and hasten his revenge,
    With your complaints unto my lord the King.
    This their dissension breeds a greater doubt.

BALTHAZAR. Assure thee Don Lorenzo he shall die,
    Or else his highness hardly shall deny.   35
    Meanwhile, I'll haste the Marshal Sessions,
    For die he shall for this his damned deed.

    Exit BALTHAZAR.

LORENZO. Why so, this fits our former policy,
    And thus experience bids the wise to deal.
    I lay the plot, he prosecutes the point,   40
    I set the trap, he breaks the worthless twigs,
    And sees not that wherewith the bird was lim'd.
    Thus hopeful men that mean to hold their own,
    Must look like fowlers to their dearest friends.
    He runs to kill whom I have holp to catch,   45
    And no man knows it was my reaching fatch.
    'Tis hard to trust unto a multitude,
    Or any one in mine opinion,
    When men themselves their secrets will reveal.

    Enter a MESSENGER *with a letter.*

    Boy!   50

PAGE. My lord.

LORENZO. What's he?

MESSENGER.   I have a letter to your lordship.

LORENZO. From whence?

MESSENGER.   From Pedringano that's imprisoned.

LORENZO. So, he is in prison then?

MESSENGER.   Ay my good lord.

LORENZO. What would he with us? He writes us here   55
  To stand good lord and help him in distress.
  Tell him I have his letters, know his mind,
  And what we may let him assure him of.
  Fellow, be gone: my boy shall follow thee.

  Exit MESSENGER.

  This works like wax, yet once more try thy wits.   60
  Boy, go convey this purse to Pedringano,
  Thou know'st the prison, closely give it him:
  And be advis'd that none be there about.
  Bid him be merry still, but secret:
  And though the Marshal Sessions be today,   65
  Bid him not doubt of his delivery.
  Tell him his pardon is already sign'd,
  And thereon bid him boldly be resolv'd:
  For were he ready to be turned off,
  As 'tis my will the uttermost be tried: 70
  Thou with his pardon shalt attend him still,
  Show him this box, tell him his pardon's in 't,
  But open 't not, and if thou lov'st thy life:
  But let him wisely keep his hopes unknown,
  He shall not want while Don Lorenzo lives: 75
  Away!

PAGE.   I go my lord, I run.

LORENZO. But sirrah, see that this be cleanly done.

Exit PAGE.

Now stands our fortune on a tickle point,
And now or never ends Lorenzo's doubts.
One only thing is unaffected yet,   80
And that's to see the executioner.
But to what end? I list not trust the air
With utterance of our pretence therein,
For fear the privy whisp'ring of the wind
Convey our words amongst unfriendly ears,   85
That lie too open to advantages.
Et quel que voglio Ii nessun le sa,
Intendo io quel mi bassara.

Exit.

Act III, Scene v

Enter BOY *with the box.*

PAGE. My master hath forbidden me to look in this box,
    and by my troth 'tis likely, if he had not warned me,
    I should not have had so much idle time: for we
    men's-kind in our minority are like women in their uncertainty,
    that they are most forbidden, they will   5
    soonest attempt: so I now. By my bare honesty here's
    nothing but the bare empty box: were it not sin against secrecy, I
    would say it were a piece of gentlemanlike
    knavery. I must go to Pedringano, and tell him his
    pardon is in this box, nay, I would have sworn it,   10
    had I not seen the contrary. I cannot choose but smile
    to think, how the villain will flout the gallows, scorn
    the audience, and descant on the hangman, and all
    presuming of his pardon from hence. Will 't not be an
    odd jest, for me to stand and grace every jest he makes, 15
    pointing my finger at this box: as who would say, 'Mock

on, here's thy warrant.' Is 't not a scurvy jest, that a man should
jest himself to death. Alas poor Pedringano, I am
in a sort sorry for thee, but if I should be hanged with
thee, I cannot weep.   20

Exit.

Act III, Scene vi

Enter HIERONIMO *and the* DEPUTY.

HIERONIMO. Thus must we toil in other men's extremes,
    That know not how to remedy our own,
    And do them justice, when unjustly we,
    For all our wrongs, can compass no redress.
    But shall I never live to see the day,   5
    That I may come (by justice of the heavens)
    To know the cause that may my cares allay?
    This toils my body, this consumeth age,
    That only I to all men just must be,
    And neither gods nor men be just to me.   10

DEPUTY. Worthy Hieronimo, your office asks
    A care to punish such as do transgress.

HIERONIMO. So is 't my duty to regard his death,
    Who when he liv'd deserv'd my dearest blood:
    But come, for that we came for let's begin,   15
    For here lies that which bids me to be gone.

    Enter OFFICERS, PAGE, [HANGMAN] *and* PEDRINGANO,
    with a letter in his hand, bound.

DEPUTY. Bring forth the prisoner for the court is set.

PEDRINGANO. Gramercy boy, but it was time to come,
    For I had written to my lord anew,
    A nearer matter that concerneth him,   20
    For fear his lordship had forgotten me:

But sith he hath remembered me so well –
Come, come, come on, when shall we to this gear.

HIERONIMO. Stand forth thou monster, murderer of men,
    And here for satisfaction of the world,   25
    Confess thy folly and repent thy fault,
    For there's thy place of execution.

PEDRINGANO. This is short work, well, to your Marshalship
    First I confess, nor fear I death therefore,
    I am the man, 'twas I slew Serberine.   30
    But sir, then you think this shall be the place,
    Where we shall satisfy you for this gear?

DEPUTY. Ay, Pedringano.

PEDRINGANO.   Now I think not so.

HIERONIMO. Peace impudent, for thou shalt find it so.
    For blood with blood, shall while I sit as judge,   35
    Be satisfied, and the law discharg'd.
    And though myself cannot receive the like,
    Yet will I see that others have their right.
    Despatch, the fault's approved and confess'd,
    And by our law he is condemn'd to die.   40

HANGMAN. Come on sir, are you ready?

PEDRINGANO. To do what, my fine officious knave?

HANGMAN. To go to this gear.

PEDRINGANO. O sir, you are too forward, thou wouldst
    fain furnish me with a halter, to disfurnish me of my   45
    habit. So I should go out of this gear my raiment, into
    that gear the rope. But hangman, now I spy your
    knavery, I'll not change without boot, that's flat.

HANGMAN. Come sir.

PEDRINGANO. So then, I must up.   50

HANGMAN. No remedy.

PEDRINGANO. Yes, but there shall be for my coming down.

HANGMAN. Indeed here's a remedy for that.

PEDRINGANO. How? Be turn'd off?

HANGMAN. Ay truly, come, are you ready. I pray sir 55
despatch, the day goes away.

PEDRINGANO. What, do you hang by the hour? If you
do, I may chance to break your old custom.

HANGMAN. Faith you have reason, for I am like to break
your young neck. 60

PEDRINGANO. Dost thou mock me hangman, pray God
I be not preserved to break your knave's pate for this.

HANGMAN. Alas sir, you are a foot too low to reach it, and
I hope you will never grow so high while I am in the office.

PEDRINGANO. Sirrah, dost see yonder boy with the box 65
in his hand?

HANGMAN. What, he that points to it with his finger?

PEDRINGANO. Ay that companion.

HANGMAN. I know him not, but what of him?

PEDRINGANO. Dost thou think to live till his old doublet 70
will make thee a new truss?

HANGMAN. Ay, and many a fair year after, to truss up
many an honester man than either thou or he.

PEDRINGANO. What hath he in his box as thou think'st?

HANGMAN. Faith I cannot tell, nor I care not greatly. Me- 75
thinks you should rather hearken to your soul's health.

PEDRINGANO. Why sirrah hangman? I take it, that that
is good for the body, is likewise good for the soul: and
it may be, in that box is balm for both.

HANGMAN. Well, thou art even the merriest piece of 80
man's flesh that e'er groaned at my office door.

PEDRINGANO. Is your roguery become an office with a
knave's name?

HANGMAN. Ay, and that shall all they witness that see you
    seal it with a thief's name.   85

PEDRINGANO. I prithee, request this good company to pray with
    me.

HANGMAN. Ay marry sir, this is a good motion: my masters, you
    see here's a good fellow.

PEDRINGANO. Nay, nay, now I remember me, let them   90
    alone till some other time, for now I have no great need.

HIERONIMO. I have not seen a wretch so impudent:
    O monstrous times where murder's set so light,
    And where the soul that should be shrin'd in heaven,
    Solely delights in interdicted things,   95
    Still wandering in the thorny passages,
    That intercepts itself of happiness.
    Murder, O bloody monster, God forbid,
    A fault so foul should 'scape unpunished.
    Despatch and see this execution done,   100
    This makes me to remember thee my son.

    Exit HIERONIMO.

PEDRINGANO. Nay soft, no haste.

DEPUTY. Why, wherefore stay you, have you hope of life?

PEDRINGANO. Why ay.

HANGMAN. As how?   105

PEDRINGANO. Why rascal by my pardon from the King.

    [*Points to the box. The* PAGE *shows it to be empty.*]

HANGMAN. Stand you on that, then you shall off with this.

    He turns him off.

DEPUTY. So executioner, convey him hence,
    But let his body be unburied.
    Let not the earth be choked or infect   110
    With that which heaven contemns and men neglect.

    Exeunt.

Act III, Scene vii

Enter HIERONIMO.

HIERONIMO. Where shall I run to breathe abroad my woes,
    My woes whose weight hath wearied the earth?
    Or mine exclaims that have surcharg'd the air
    With ceaseless plaints for my deceased son?
    The blust'ring winds conspiring with my words,   5
    At my lament have mov'd the leafless trees,
    Disrob'd the meadows of their flowered green,
    Made mountains marsh with spring tides of my tears,
    And broken through the brazen gates of hell,
    Yet still tormented is my tortured soul   10
    With broken sighs and restless passions,
    That winged mount, and hovering in the air,
    Beat at the windows of the brightest heavens,
    Soliciting for justice and revenge:
    But they are plac'd in those imperial heights,   15
    Where countermur'd with walls of diamond,
    I find the place impregnable, and they
    Resist my woes, and give my words no way.

Enter HANGMAN *with a letter.*

HANGMAN. O lord sir, God bless you sir, the man Sir
    Petergade, sir, he that was so full of merry conceits –   20

HIERONIMO. Well, what of him?

HANGMAN. O lord sir, he went the wrong way, the fellow
    had a fair commission to the contrary. Sir, here is his passport, I
    pray you sir, we have done him wrong.

HIERONIMO. I warrant thee, give it me.   25

HANGMAN. You will stand between the gallows and me.

HIERONIMO. Ay, ay.

HANGMAN. I thank your lord worship.

    Exit HANGMAN.

HIERONIMO. And yet though somewhat nearer me concerns,
   I will to ease the grief that I sustain,   30
   Take truce with sorrow while I read on this.
   'My lord, I write as mine extremes requir'd,
   That you would labour my delivery:
   If you neglect, my life is desperate,
   And in my death I shall reveal the troth.   35
   You know my lord, I slew him for your sake,
   And was confederate with the Prince and you,
   Won by rewards and hopeful promises,
   I holp to murder Don Horatio too.'
   Holp he to murder mine Horatio,   40
   And actors in th' accursed tragedy
   Wast thou Lorenzo, Balthazar and thou,
   Of whom my son, my son deserv'd so well,
   What have I heard, what have mine eyes beheld?
   O sacred heavens, may it come to pass,   45
   That such a monstrous and detested deed,
   So closely smothered, and so long conceal'd,
   Shall thus by this be venged or reveal'd.
   Now see I what I durst not then suspect,
   That Bel-imperia's letter was not feign'd,   50
   Nor feigned she though falsely they have wrong'd
   Both her, myself, Horatio, and themselves.
   Now may I make compare 'twixt hers and this,
   Of every accident, I ne'er could find
   Till now, and now I feelingly perceive,   55
   They did what heaven unpunish'd would not leave.
   O false Lorenzo, are these thy flattering looks?
   Is this the honour that thou didst my son?
   And Balthazar bane to thy soul and me,
   Was this the ransom he reserv'd thee for?   60
   Woe to the cause of these constrained wars,
   Woe to thy baseness and captivity,
   Woe to thy birth, thy body and thy soul,
   Thy cursed father, and thy conquer'd self:
   And bann'd with bitter execrations be   65
   The day and place where he did pity thee.

But wherefore waste I mine unfruitful words?
When naught but blood will satisfy my woes:
I will go plain me to my lord the King,
And cry aloud for justice through the Court,   70
Wearing the flints with these my withered feet,
And either purchase justice by entreats,
Or tire them all with my revenging threats.

Exit.

Act III, Scene viii

Enter ISABELLA *and her* MAID.

ISABELLA. So that you say this herb will purge the eye
    And this the head.
    Ah but none of them will purge the heart:
    No, there's no medicine left for my disease,
    Nor any physic to recure the dead.   5

    She runs lunatic.

    Horatio, O, where's Horatio?

MAID. Good madame, affright not thus yourself,
    With outrage for your son Horatio.
    He sleeps in quiet in the Elysian fields.   9

ISABELLA. Why did I not give you gowns and goodly things,
    Bought you a whistle and a whipstalk too:
    To be revenged on their villainies.

MAID. Madame these humours do torment my soul.

ISABELLA. My soul, poor soul thou talks of things
    Thou know'st not what, my soul hath silver wings,   15
    That mounts me up unto the highest heavens,
    To heaven, ay there sits my Horatio,
    Back'd with a troupe of fiery cherubins,

Dancing about his newly healed wounds
Singing sweet hymns and chanting heavenly notes,   20
Rare harmony to greet his innocence,
That died, ay died a mirror in our days.
But say, where shall I find, the men, the murderers,
That slew Horatio, whither shall I run,
To find them out, that murdered my son?   25

Exeunt.

Act III, Scene ix

BEL-IMPERIA *at a window.*

BEL-IMPERIA. What means this outrage that is offer'd me?
    Why am I thus sequester'd from the Court?
    No notice, shall I not know the cause
    Of this my secret and suspicious ills?
    Accursed brother, unkind murderer: 5
    Why bends thou thus thy mind to martyr me?
    Hieronimo, why writ I of thy wrongs?
    Or why art thou so slack in thy revenge?
    Andrea, O Andrea that thou sawest,
    Me for thy friend Horatio handled thus,   10
    And him for me thus causeless murdered.
    Well, force perforce, I must constrain myself,
    To patience, and apply me to the time,
    Till heaven as I have hop'd shall set me free.   14

Enter CHRISTOPHIL.

CHRISTOPHIL. Come, Madame Bel-imperia, this may not be.

Exeunt.

Act III, Scene x

Enter LORENZO, BALTHAZAR, *and the* PAGE.

LORENZO. Boy, talk no further, thus far things go well,
    Thou art assured that thou sawest him dead?

PAGE. Or else my lord I live not.

LORENZO.   That's enough.
    As for his resolution in his end,
    Leave that to him with whom he sojourns now.   5
    Here, take my ring, and give it Christophil,
    And bid him let my sister be enlarg'd,
    And bring her hither straight.

    Exit PAGE.

    This that I did was for a policy,
    To smooth and keep the murder secret,   10
    Which as a nine days' wonder being o'erblown,
    My gentle sister will I now enlarge.

BALTHAZAR. And time Lorenzo, for my lord the Duke,
    You heard enquired for her yester-night.

LORENZO. Why, and my lord, I hope you heard me say,   15
    Sufficient reason, why she kept away.
    But that's all one, my lord, you love her?

BALTHAZAR.   Ay.

LORENZO. Then in your love beware, deal cunningly,
    Salve all suspicions, only soothe me up,
    And if she hap to stand on terms with us,   20
    As for her sweetheart, and concealment so,
    Jest with her gently, under feigned jest
    Are things conceal'd, that else would breed unrest.
    But here she comes.

    Enter BEL-IMPERIA.

                Now, sister –

BEL-IMPERIA.   Sister, no,
    Thou art no brother, but an enemy.   25

Else wouldst thou not have us'd thy sister so,
First, to affright me with thy weapons drawn,
And with extremes abuse my company:
And then to hurry me like whirlwind's rage,
Amidst a crew of thy confederates: 30
And clap me up where none might come at me,
Nor I at any to reveal my wrongs.
What madding fury did possess thy wits?
Or wherein is 't that I offended thee?

LORENZO. Advise you better Bel-imperia,   35
  For I have done you no disparagement:
  Unless by more discretion than deserv'd,
  I sought to save your honour and mine own.

BEL-IMPERIA. Mine honour, why Lorenzo, wherein is 't,
  That I neglect my reputation so,   40
  As you, or any need to rescue it.

LORENZO. His highness and my father were resolv'd
  To come confer with old Hieronimo,
  Concerning certain matters of estate,
  That by the Viceroy was determined.   45

BEL-IMPERIA. And wherein was mine honour touch'd in that?

BALTHAZAR. Have patience Bel-imperia, hear the rest.

LORENZO. Me next in sight as messenger they sent,
  To give him notice that they were so nigh:
  Now when I came consorted with the Prince,   50
  And unexpected in an arbour there,
  Found Bel-imperia with Horatio.

BEL-IMPERIA. How then?

LORENZO. Why then remembering that old disgrace,
  Which you for Don Andrea had endur'd,   55
  And now were likely longer to sustain,
  By being found so meanly accompanied:
  Thought rather, for I knew no readier mean,
  To thrust Horatio forth my father's way.

BALTHAZAR. And carry you obscurely somewhere else,   60
  Lest that his highness should have found you there.

BEL-IMPERIA. Even so my lord, and you are witness,
  That this is true which he entreateth of?
  You (gentle brother) forg'd this for my sake,
  And you my lord, were made his instrument: 65
  A work of worth, worthy the noting too.
  But what's the cause that you conceal'd me since?

LORENZO. Your melancholy sister since the news
  Of your first favourite Don Andrea's death,
  My father's old wrath hath exasperate.   70

BALTHAZAR. And better was 't for you being in disgrace,
  To absent yourself and give his fury place.

BEL-IMPERIA. But why had I no notice of his ire?

LORENZO. That were to add more fuel to your fire,
  Who burnt like Aetna for Andrea's loss.   75

BEL-IMPERIA. Hath not my father then enquir'd for me?

LORENZO. Sister he hath, and thus excus'd I thee.

He whispereth in her ear.

  But Bel-imperia, see the gentle prince,
  Look on thy love, behold young Balthazar,
  Whose passions by thy presence are increas'd,   80
  And in whose melancholy thou may'st see
  Thy hate, his love: thy flight, his following thee.

BEL-IMPERIA. Brother you are become an orator,
  I know not I, by what experience,
  Too politic for me, past all compare,   85
  Since last I saw you, but content yourself,
  The Prince is meditating higher things.

BALTHAZAR. 'Tis of thy beauty then that conquers kings.
  Of those thy tresses Ariadne's twines,
  Wherewith my liberty thou hast surpris'd.   90
  Of that thine ivory front my sorrow's map,
  Wherein I see no haven to rest my hope.

BEL-IMPERIA. To love, and fear, and both at once my lord,
    In my conceit, are things of more import
    Than women's wits are to be busied with.   95

BALTHAZAR. 'Tis I that love.

BEL-IMPERIA.   Whom?

BALTHAZAR.   Bel-imperia.

BEL-IMPERIA. But I that fear.

BALTHAZAR.   Whom?

BEL-IMPERIA.   Bel-imperia.

LORENZO. Fear yourself?

BEL-IMPERIA.   Ay brother.

LORENZO.   How?

BEL-IMPERIA.   As those,
    That what they love, are loath, and fear to lose.

BALTHAZAR. Then fair, let Balthazar your keeper be.   100

BEL-IMPERIA. No, Balthazar doth fear as well as we.
    Est tremulo metui pavidum junxere timorem,
    Et vanum stolidae proditionis opus.

    Exit.

LORENZO. Nay, and you argue things so cunningly,
    We'll go continue this discourse at Court.   105

BALTHAZAR. Led by the loadstar of her heavenly looks,
    Wends poor oppressed Balthazar,
    As o'er the mountains walks the wanderer,
    Incertain to effect his pilgrimage.

    Exeunt.

Act III, Scene xi

Enter two PORTINGALES, *and* HIERONIMO *meets them.*

FIRST PORTINGALE. By your leave sir.

HIERONIMO. Good leave have you, nay, I pray you go,
    For I'll leave you, if you can leave me so.

SECOND PORTINGALE. Pray you, which is the next way
    to my lord the Duke's?

HIERONIMO. The next way from me.

FIRST PORTINGALE. To his house we mean.   5

HIERONIMO. O hard by, 'tis yon house that you see.

SECOND PORTINGALE. You could not tell us, if his son
    were there.

HIERONIMO. Who, my lord Lorenzo?

FIRST PORTINGALE.   Ay, sir.

He goeth in at one door and comes out at another.

HIERONIMO.   O forbear,
    For other talk for us far fitter were.
    But if you be importunate to know,   10
    The way to him, and where to find him out,
    Then list to me, and I'll resolve your doubt,
    There is a path upon your left hand side,
    That leadeth from a guilty conscience,
    Unto a forest of distrust and fear.   15
    A darksome place and dangerous to pass,
    There shall you meet with melancholy thoughts,
    Whose baleful humours if you but uphold,
    It will conduct you to despair and death:
    Whose rocky cliffs, when you have once beheld,   20
    Within a hugy dale of lasting night,
    That kindled with the world's iniquities,
    Doth cast up filthy and detested fumes.
    Not far from thence where murderers have built,

A habitation for their cursed souls: 25
There in a brazen cauldron fix'd by Jove
In his fell wrath upon a sulphur flame:
Your selves shall find Lorenzo bathing him,
In boiling lead and blood of innocents.

FIRST PORTINGALE. Ha, ha, ha.

HIERONIMO.   Ha, ha, ha: 30
Why, ha, ha, ha. Farewell, good, ha, ha, ha.

Exit.

SECOND PORTINGALE. Doubtless this man is passing lunatic,
Or imperfection of his age doth make him dote.
Come, let's away to seek my lord the Duke.

[*Exeunt.*]

Act III, Scene xii

Enter HIERONIMO *with a poniard in one hand, and a rope in the other.*

HIERONIMO. Now sir, perhaps I come and see the King,
The King sees me, and fain would hear my suit.
Why is not this a strange and seld seen thing,
That standers by with toys should strike me mute.
Go to, I see their shifts, and say no more,   5
Hieronimo, 'tis time for thee to trudge.
Down by the dale that flows with purple gore,
Standeth a fiery tower, there sits a judge,
Upon a seat of steel and molten brass:
And 'twixt his teeth he holds a fire-brand,   10
That leads unto the lake where hell doth stand.
Away Hieronimo to him be gone:
He'll do thee justice for Horatio's death.
Turn down this path, thou shalt be with him straight,
Or this, and then thou need'st not take thy breath.   15
This way, or that way: soft and fair, not so:

For if I hang or kill myself, let's know
Who will revenge Horatio's murder then?
No, no, fie no: pardon me, I'll none of that.

He flings away the dagger and halter.

This way I'll take, and this way comes the King,   20

He takes them up again.

And here I'll have a fling at him, that's flat.
And Balthazar I'll be with thee to bring,
And thee Lorenzo, here's the King, nay, stay,
And here, ay here, there goes the hare away.

Enter KING, AMBASSADOR, CASTILE, *and* LORENZO.

KING. Now show Ambassador what our Viceroy saith,   25
　　Hath he receiv'd the articles we sent?

HIERONIMO. Justice, O justice to Hieronimo.

LORENZO. Back, see'st thou not the King is busy?

HIERONIMO. O, is he so?

KING. Who is he that interrupts our business?   30

HIERONIMO. Not I, Hieronimo beware, go by, go by.

AMBASSADOR. Renowned King, he hath receiv'd and read
　　Thy kingly proffers, and thy promis'd league,
　　And as a man extremely overjoy'd,
　　To hear his son so princely entertain'd,   35
　　Whose death he had so solemnly bewail'd.
　　This for thy further satisfaction,
　　And kingly love, he kindly lets thee know:
　　First, for the marriage of his princely son,
　　With Bel-imperia thy beloved niece,   40
　　The news are more delightful to his soul,
　　Than myrrh or incense to the offended heavens.
　　In person therefore will he come himself,
　　To see the marriage rites solemnised,
　　And, in the presence of the Court of Spain,   45
　　To knit a sure inexplicable band
　　Of kingly love, and everlasting league,

Betwixt the crowns of Spain and Portingale.
There will he give his crown to Balthazar,
And make a Queen of Bel-imperia.   50

KING. Brother, how like you this our Viceroy's love?

CASTILE. No doubt my lord, it is an argument
Of honourable care to keep his friend,
And wondrous zeal to Balthazar his son?
Nor am I least indebted to his grace,   55
That bends his liking to my daughter thus.

AMBASSADOR. Now last (dread lord) here hath his highness sent,
Although he send not that his son return,
His ransom due to Don Horatio.

HIERONIMO. Horatio, who calls Horatio?   60

KING. And well rememb'red, thank his majesty.
Here, see it given to Horatio.

HIERONIMO. Justice, O justice, justice, gentle King.

KING. Who is that? Hieronimo?

HIERONIMO. Justice, O, justice! O my son, my son,   65
My son whom naught can ransom or redeem.

LORENZO. Hieronimo, you are not well advis'd.

HIERONIMO. Away Lorenzo hinder me no more,
For thou hast made me bankrupt of my bliss:
Give me my son, you shall not ransom him.   70
Away, I'll rip the bowels of the earth,

He diggeth with his dagger.

And ferry over to th' Elysian plains,
And bring my son to show his deadly wounds.
Stand from about me,
I'll make a pickaxe of my poniard,   75
And here surrender up my Marshalship:
For I'll go marshal up the fiends in hell,
To be avenged on you all for this.

KING. What means this outrage?
      Will none of you restrain his fury?   80

HIERONIMO. Nay soft and fair, you shall not need to strive,
      Needs must he go that the devils drive.

      Exit.

KING. What accident hath happ'd Hieronimo?
      I have not seen him to demean him so.

LORENZO. My gracious lord, he is with extreme pride,   85
      Conceiv'd of young Horatio his son,
      And covetous of having to himself
      The ransom of the young Prince Balthazar,
      Distract and in a manner lunatic.

KING. Believe me nephew we are sorry for 't,   90
      This is the love that fathers bear their sons:
      But gentle brother, go give to him this gold,
      The Prince's ransom, let him have his due,
      For what he hath Horatio shall not want,
      Haply Hieronimo hath need thereof.   95

LORENZO. But if he be thus helplessly distract,
      'Tis requisite his office be resign'd,
      And given to one of more discretion.

KING. We shall increase his melancholy so.
      'Tis best that we see further in it first: 100
      Till when, ourself will exempt the place.
      And brother, now bring in the Ambassador,
      That he may be a witness of the match
      'Twixt Balthazar and Bel-imperia,
      And that we may prefix a certain time,   105
      Wherein the marriage shall be solemnis'd,
      That we may have thy lord the Viceroy here.

AMBASSADOR. Therein your highness highly shall content
      His majesty, that longs to hear from hence.

KING. On, then, and hear you Lord Ambassador.   110

      Exeunt.

Act III, Scene xiii

Enter HIERONIMO *with a book in his hand.*

HIERONIMO. *Vindicta mihi.*
    Ay, heaven will be reveng'd of every ill,
    Nor will they suffer murder unrepaid:
    Then stay Hieronimo, attend their will,
    For mortal men may not appoint their time. 5
    Per scelus semper tutum est sceleribus iter.
    Strike, and strike home, where wrong is offer'd thee,
    For evils unto ills conductors be,
    And death's the worst of resolution.
    For he that thinks with patience to contend 10
    To quiet life, his life shall easily end.
    Fata si miseros juvant, habes salutem:
    Fata si vitam negant, habes sepulchrum.
    If destiny thy miseries do ease,
    Then hast thou health, and happy shalt thou be: 15
    If destiny deny thee life Hieronimo,
    Yet shalt thou be assured of a tomb:
    If neither, yet let this thy comfort be,
    Heaven covereth him that hath no burial,
    And to conclude, I will revenge his death, 20
    But how? Not as the vulgar wits of men,
    With open, but inevitable ills:
    As by a secret, yet a certain mean,
    Which under kindship will be cloaked best.
    Wise men will take their opportunity, 25
    Closely and safely fitting things to time:
    But in extremes advantage hath no time.
    And therefore all times fit not for revenge:
    Thus therefore will I rest me in unrest,
    Dissembling quiet in unquietness, 30
    Not seeming that I know their villainies:
    That my simplicity may make them think,
    That ignorantly I will let all slip:
    For ignorance I wot, and well they know,
    Remedium malorum iners est. 35

Nor aught avails it me to menace them,
Who as a wintry storm upon a plain,
Will bear me down with their nobility.
No, no, Hieronimo, thou must enjoin
Thine eyes to observation, and thy tongue   40
To milder speeches, than thy spirit affords,
Thy heart to patience, and thy hands to rest,
Thy cap to courtesy, and thy knee to bow,
Till to revenge thou know, when, where, and how.
How now, what noise, what coil is that you keep?   45

A noise within. Enter a SERVANT.

SERVANT. Here are a sort of poor petitioners,
That are importunate and it shall please you sir,
That you should plead their cases to the King.

HIERONIMO. That I should plead their several actions,
Why let them enter, and let me see them.   50

Enter three CITIZENS *and an old man* [BAZULTO].

FIRST CITIZEN. So I tell you this for learning and for law,
There's not any advocate in Spain,
That can prevail, or will take half the pain,
That he will in pursuit of equity.

HIERONIMO. Come near you men that thus importune me. 55
[*Aside.*] Now must I bear a face of gravity,
For thus I us'd before my Marshalship,
To plead in causes as Corregidor.
Come on sirs, what's the matter?

SECOND CITIZEN.   Sir, an action.

HIERONIMO. Of battery?

FIRST CITIZEN.   Mine of debt.

HIERONIMO.   Give place.   60

SECOND CITIZEN. No sir, mine is an action of the case.

THIRD CITIZEN. Mine an *ejectione firma* by a lease.

HIERONIMO. Content you sirs, are you determined,
     That I should plead your several actions?

FIRST CITIZEN. Ay sir, and here's my declaration.   65

SECOND CITIZEN. And here is my band.

THIRD CITIZEN.   And here is my lease.

They give him papers.

HIERONIMO. But wherefore stands yon silly man so mute,
     With mournful eyes and hands to heaven uprear'd?
     Come hither father, let me know thy cause.

BAZULTO. O worthy sir my cause, but slightly known,   70
     May move the hearts of warlike myrmidons,
     And melt the Corsic rocks with ruthful tears.

HIERONIMO. Say father, tell me what's thy suit?

BAZULTO. No, sir could my woes
     Give way unto my most distressful words,   75
     Then should I not in paper as you see,
     With ink bewray, what blood began in me.

HIERONIMO. What's here? 'The humble supplication
     Of Don Bazulto for his murd'red son.'

BAZULTO. Ay sir.

IIIERONIMO.   No sir, it was my murd'red son,   80
     O my son. My son, O my son Horatio!
     But mine, or thine, Bazulto be content.
     Here, take my hand-kercher and wipe thine eyes,
     Whiles wretched I, in thy mishaps may see,
     The lively portrait of my dying self.   85

He draweth out a bloody napkin.

     O no, not this, Horatio this was thine,
     And when I dyed it in thy dearest blood,
     This was a token 'twixt thy soul and me,
     That of thy death revenged I should be.
     But here, take this, and this, what my purse?   90

Ay this and that, and all of them are thine,
For all as one are our extremities.

FIRST CITIZEN. Oh, see the kindness of Hieronimo.

SECOND CITIZEN. This gentleness shows him a gentleman.

HIERONIMO. See, see, oh see thy shame Hieronimo,   95
   See here a loving father to his son:
   Behold the sorrows and the sad laments,
   That he delivereth for his son's decease.
   If love's effects so strives in lesser things,
   If love enforce such moods in meaner wits,   100
   If love express such power in poor estates:
   Hieronimo, when as a raging sea,
   Toss'd with the wind and tide o'erturneth then
   The upper billows course of waves to keep,
   Whilst lesser waters labour in the deep.   105
   Then sham'st thou not Hieronimo to neglect
   The sweet revenge of thy Horatio.
   Though on this earth justice will not be found:
   I'll down to hell, and in this passion,
   Knock at the dismal gates of Pluto's court,   110
   Getting by force as once Alcides did,
   A troupe of furies and tormenting hags,
   To torture Don Lorenzo and the rest.
   Yet least the triple headed porter should
   Deny my passage to the slimy strond,   115
   The Thracian poet thou shalt counterfeit:
   Come on old father be my Orpheus,
   And if thou canst no notes upon the harp,
   Then sound the burden of thy sore heart's grief,
   Till we do gain that Proserpine may grant   120
   Revenge on them that murdered my son,
   Then will I rent and tear them thus and thus,
   Shivering their limbs in pieces with my teeth.

   Tear the papers.

FIRST CITIZEN. O sir my declaration.

   Exit HIERONIMO *and they after.*

SECOND CITIZEN. Save my bond.   125

   Enter HIERONIMO.

   Save my bond.

THIRD CITIZEN. Alas my lease, it cost me ten pound,
   And you my lord have torn the same.

HIERONIMO. That cannot be, I gave it never a wound,
   Show me one drop of blood fall from the same: 130
   How is it possible I should slay it then,
   Tush no, run after, catch me if you can.

   Exeunt all but the old man. BAZULTO *remains till* HIERONIMO
   enters again, who staring him in the face speaks.

HIERONIMO. And art thou come Horatio from the depth,
   To ask for justice in this upper earth?
   To tell thy father thou art unreveng'd,   135
   To wring more tears from Isabella's eyes?
   Whose lights are dimm'd with over-long laments.
   Go back my son, complain to Aeacus,
   For here's no justice, gentle boy be gone.
   For justice is exiled from the earth: 140
   Hieronimo will bear thee company.
   Thy mother cries on righteous Rhadamanth,
   For just revenge against the murderers.

BAZULTO. Alas my lord, whence springs this troubled speech?

HIERONIMO. But let me look on my Horatio: 145
   Sweet boy how art thou chang'd in death's black shade?
   Had Proserpine no pity on thy youth?
   But suffer'd thy fair crimson colour'd spring,
   With withered winter to be blasted thus?
   Horatio, thou art older than thy father: 150
   Ah ruthless father, that favour thus transforms?

BAZULTO. Ah my good lord, I am not your young son.

HIERONIMO. What, not my son, thou then a fury art,
   Sent from the empty kingdom of black night,

To summon me to make appearance   155
Before grim Minos and just Rhadamanth.
To plague Hieronimo that is remiss,
And seeks not vengeance for Horatio's death.

BAZULTO. I am a grieved man and not a ghost,
That came for justice for my murdered son.   160

HIERONIMO. Ay, now I know thee, now thou nam'st thy son,
Thou art the lively image of my grief,
Within thy face, my sorrows I may see.
Thy eyes are gumm'd with tears, thy cheeks are wan,
Thy forehead troubled, and thy muttering lips   165
Murmur sad words abruptly broken off,
By force of windy sighs thy spirit breathes,
And all this sorrow riseth for thy son:
And self same sorrow feel I for my son.
Come in old man, thou shalt to Isabel,   170
Lean on my arm, I thee, thou me shalt stay,
And thou, and I, and she will sing a song:
Three parts in one, but all of discords fram'd,
Talk not of cords, but let us now be gone,
For with a cord Horatio was slain.   175

Exeunt.

Act III, Scene xiv

Enter KING *of Spain,* CASTILE, VICEROY, *and* LORENZO,
BALTHAZAR, DON PEDRO, *and* BEL-IMPERIA.

KING. Go brother it is the Duke of Castile's cause,
Salute the viceroy in our name.

CASTILE.   I go.

VICEROY. Go forth Don Pedro for thy nephew's sake,
And greet the Duke of Castile.

PEDRO.   It shall be so.

KING. And now to meet these Portuguese,   5
    For as we now are, so sometimes were these,
    Kings and commanders of the western Indies.
    Welcome brave Viceroy to the Court of Spain,
    And welcome all his honourable train:
    'Tis not unknown to us, for why you come,   10
    Or have so kingly cross'd the seas:
    Sufficeth it in this we note the troth,
    And more than common love you lend to us.
    So is it that mine honourable niece,
    For it beseems us now that it be known,   15
    Already is betroth'd to Balthazar:
    And by appointment and our condescent,
    Tomorrow are they to be married.
    To this intent we entertain thyself,
    Thy followers, their pleasure, and our peace: 20
    Speak men of Portingale, shall it be so?
    If ay, say so: if not, say flatly no.

VICEROY. Renowned King, I come not as thou think'st,
    With doubtful followers, unresolved men,
    But such as have upon thine articles,   25
    Confirm'd thy motion and contented me.
    Know sovereign, I come to solemnise
    The marriage of thy beloved niece,
    Fair Bel-imperia, with my Balthazar.
    With thee my son, whom sith I live to see.   30
    Here take my crown, I give it her and thee,
    And let me live a solitary life,
    In ceaseless prayers,
    To think how strangely heaven hath thee preserv'd.

KING. See brother, see, how nature strives in him,   35
    Come worthy Viceroy and accompany
    Thy friend, with thine extremities:
    A place more private fits this princely mood.

VICEROY. Or here or where your highness thinks it good.

    Exeunt all but CASTILE *and* LORENZO.

CASTILE. Nay stay Lorenzo, let me talk with you,   40
  See'st thou this entertainment of these kings?

LORENZO. I do my lord, and joy to see the same.

CASTILE. And knowest thou why this meeting is?

LORENZO. For her my lord, whom Balthazar doth love,
  And to confirm their promis'd marriage.   45

CASTILE. She is thy sister?

LORENZO.   Who, Bel-imperia?
  Ay my gracious lord, and this is the day,
  That I have long'd so happily to see.

CASTILE. Thou wouldst be loath that any fault of thine
  Should intercept her in her happiness.   50

LORENZO. Heavens will not let Lorenzo err so much.

CASTILE. Why then Lorenzo listen to my words:
  It is suspected and reported too,
  That thou Lorenzo wrong'st Hieronimo,
  And in his suits towards his majesty,   55
  Still keep'st him back, and seeks to cross his suit.

LORENZO. That I my lord?

CASTILE. I tell thee son myself have heard it said,
  When to my sorrow I have been asham'd
  To answer for thee, though thou art my son.   60
  Lorenzo, knowest thou not the common love,
  And kindness that Hieronimo hath won,
  By his deserts within the Court of Spain?
  Or seest thou not the King my brother's care,
  In his behalf, and to procure his health?   65
  Lorenzo, shouldst thou thwart his passions,
  And he exclaim against thee to the King,
  What honour were 't in this assembly,
  Or what a scandal were 't among the kings,
  To hear Hieronimo exclaim on thee.   70
  Tell me, and look thou tell me truly too,
  Whence grows the ground of this report in Court.

LORENZO. My lord, it lies not in Lorenzo's power,
    To stop the vulgar, liberal of their tongues:
    A small advantage makes a water breach, 75
    And no man lives that long contenteth all.

CASTILE. Myself have seen thee busy to keep back
    Him and his supplications from the King.

LORENZO. Yourself my lord hath seen his passions,
    That ill beseem'd the presence of a King, 80
    And for I pitied him in his distress,
    I held him thence with kind and courteous words,
    As free from malice to Hieronimo
    As to my soul, my lord.

CASTILE. Hieronimo my son, mistakes thee then. 85

LORENZO. My gracious father, believe me so he doth,
    But what's a silly man distract in mind
    To think upon the murder of his son:
    Alas, how easy is it for him to err?
    But for his satisfaction and the world's, 90
    'Twere good my lord that Hieronimo and I
    Were reconciled, if he misconster me.

CASTILE. Lorenzo thou hast said, it shall be so,
    Go one of you and call Hieronimo.

Enter BALTHAZAR *and* BEL-IMPERIA.

BALTHAZAR. Come Bel-imperia, Balthazar's content, 95
    My sorrow's ease and sovereign of my bliss,
    Sith heaven hath ordain'd thee to be mine:
    Disperse those clouds and melancholy looks,
    And clear them up with those thy sun bright eyes,
    Wherein my hope and heaven's fair beauty lies. 100

BEL-IMPERIA. My looks my lord, are fitting for my love,
    Which new begun, can show no brighter yet.

BALTHAZAR. New kindled flames should burn as morning sun.

BEL-IMPERIA. But not too fast, lest heat and all be done.
    I see my lord my father.

BALTHAZAR.   Truce my love,   105
  I will go salute him.

CASTILE.   Welcome Balthazar,
  Welcome brave Prince, the pledge of Castile's peace:
  And welcome Bel-imperia, how now girl?
  Why com'st thou sadly to salute us thus?
  Content thyself for I am satisfied,   110
  It is not now as when Andrea liv'd,
  We have forgotten and forgiven that,
  And thou art graced with a happier love,
  But Balthazar here comes Hieronimo.
  I'll have a word with him.   115

  Enter HIERONIMO *and a* SERVANT.

HIERONIMO. And where's the Duke?

SERVANT.   Yonder.

HIERONIMO.   Even so:
  What new device have they devised trow?
  Pocas palabras, mild as the lamb,
  Is 't I will be reveng'd? No, I am not the man.

CASTILE. Welcome Hieronimo.   120

LORENZO. Welcome Hieronimo.

BALTHAZAR. Welcome Hieronimo.

HIERONIMO. My lords I thank you for Horatio.

CASTILE. Hieronimo, the reason that I sent
  To speak with you, is this.

HIERONIMO.   What, so short?   125
  Then I'll be gone, I thank you for 't.

CASTILE. Nay, stay Hieronimo, go call him son.

LORENZO. Hieronimo, my father craves a word with you.

HIERONIMO. With me sir? Why my lord I thought you
     had done.

LORENZO [*aside*]. No, would he had.

CASTILE.   Hieronimo, I hear   130
  You find yourself aggrieved at my son,
  Because you have not access unto the King,
  And say 'tis he that intercepts your suits.

HIERONIMO. Why, is not this a miserable thing my lord?

CASTILE. Hieronimo, I hope you have no cause,   135
  And would be loath that one of your deserts
  Should once have reason to suspect my son,
  Considering how I think of you myself.

HIERONIMO. Your son Lorenzo, whom, my noble lord?
  The hope of Spain, mine honourable friend?   140
  Grant me the combat of them, if they dare.

  Draws out his sword.

  I'll meet him face to face to tell me so.
  These be the scandalous reports of such,
  As loves not me, and hate my lord too much,
  Should I suspect Lorenzo would prevent,   145
  Or cross my suit, that lov'd my son so well.
  My lord, I am asham'd it should be said.

LORENZO. Hieronimo, I never gave you cause.

HIERONIMO. My good lord, I know you did not.

CASTILE.   There then pause,
  And for the satisfaction of the world,   150
  Hieronimo frequent my homely house,
  The Duke of Castile Cyprian's ancient seat,
  And when thou wilt, use me, my son, and it:
  But here before Prince Balthazar and me,
  Embrace each other, and be perfect friends.   155

HIERONIMO. Ay marry my lord, and shall:
  Friends (quoth he) see, I'll be friends with you all.
  Specially with you my lovely lord,
  For divers causes it is fit for us,

That we be friends, the world is suspicious,   160
And men may think what we imagine not.

BALTHAZAR. Why this is friendly done Hieronimo.

LORENZO. And that I hope old grudges are forgot.

HIERONIMO. What else, it were a shame it should not be so.

CASTILE. Come on Hieronimo at my request,   165
Let us intreat your company today.

Exeunt [all but HIERONIMO].

HIERONIMO. Your lordship's to command. Pha: keep your way.
Mi. Chi mi fa? Pui corezze che non sule
Tradito viha, otrada vule.

Exit.

Act III, Scene xv

GHOST [*of Andrea*] *and* REVENGE.

GHOST. Awake Erichtho! Cerberus awake,
Solicit Pluto gentle Proserpine,
To combat Acheron and Erebus in hell.
For ne'er by Styx and Phlegethon,
Nor ferried Charon to the fiery lakes,   5
Such fearful sights, as poor Andrea sees?
Revenge awake!

REVENGE.   Awake, for why?

ANDREA. Awake Revenge, for thou art ill advis'd,
To sleep away, what thou art warn'd to watch.

REVENGE. Content thyself, and do not trouble me.   10

ANDREA. Awake Revenge, if love, as love hath had,
Have yet the power or prevalence in hell,
Hieronimo with Lorenzo is joined in league,

And intercepts our passage to revenge:
Awake Revenge, or we are woe begone.   15

REVENGE. Thus worldlings ground what they have
    dream'd upon.
  Content thyself Andrea, though I sleep,
  Yet is my mood soliciting their souls,
  Sufficeth thee that poor Hieronimo
  Cannot forget his son Horatio.   20
  Nor dies Revenge although he sleep a while,
  For in unquiet, quietness is feign'd:
  And slumb'ring is a common worldly wile.
  Behold Andrea for an instance how
  Revenge hath slept, and then imagine thou,   25
  What 'tis to be subject to destiny.

Enter a dumb show. [They perform and leave.]

ANDREA. Awake Revenge, reveal this mystery.

REVENGE. The two first the nuptial torches bore,
  As brightly burning as the mid-day's sun:
  But after them doth Hymen hie as fast,   30
  Clothed in sable, and a saffron robe,
  And blows them out, and quencheth them with blood,
  As discontent that things continue so.

ANDREA. Sufficeth me thy meaning's understood,
  And thanks to thee and those infernal powers,   35
  That will not tolerate a lover's woe.
  Rest thee, for I will sit to see the rest.

REVENGE. Then argue not, for thou hast thy request.

Exeunt.

Act IV, Scene i

Enter BEL-IMPERIA *and* HIERONIMO.

BEL-IMPERIA. Is this the love thou bear'st Horatio?
   Is this the kindness that thou counterfeits,
   Are these the fruits of thine incessant tears?
   Hieronimo, are these thy passions?
   Thy protestations, and thy deep laments,   5
   That thou wert wont to weary men withal?
   O unkind father, O deceitful world,
   With what excuses canst thou show thyself?
   With what dishonour, and the hate of men,
   From this dishonour and the hate of men.   10
   Thus to neglect the loss and life of him,
   Whom both my letters, and thine own belief,
   Assures thee to be causeless slaughtered.
   Hieronimo, for shame Hieronimo:
   Be not a history to after times,   15
   Of such ingratitude unto thy son.
   Unhappy mothers of such children then,
   But monstrous fathers, to forget so soon
   The death of those, whom they with care and cost
   Have tender'd so, thus careless should be lost.   20
   Myself a stranger in respect of thee,
   So loved his life, as still I wish their deaths,
   Nor shall his death be unreveng'd by me,
   Although I bear it out for fashion's sake:
   For here I swear in sight of heaven and earth,   25
   Shouldst thou neglect the love thou shouldst retain,
   And give it over and devise no more,
   Myself should send their hateful souls to hell,
   That wrought his downfall with extremest death.

HIERONIMO. But may it be that Bel-imperia   30
    Vows such revenge as she hath deign'd to say:
    Why then I see that heaven applies our drift,
    And all the saints do sit soliciting
    For vengeance on those cursed murderers.
    Madame 'tis true, and now I find it so,   35
    I found a letter, written in your name,
    And in that letter, how Horatio died.
    Pardon, O pardon, Bel-imperia,
    My fear and care in not believing it,
    Nor think, I thoughtless think upon a mean,   40
    To let his death be unreveng'd at full,
    And here I vow, so you but give consent,
    And will conceal my resolution,
    I will ere long determine of their deaths,
    That causeless thus have murdered my son.   45

BEL-IMPERIA. Hieronimo, I will consent, conceal,
    And aught that may effect for thine avail,
    Join with thee to revenge Horatio's death.

HIERONIMO. On then, whatsoever I devise,
    Let me entreat you grace my practices.   50
    For why, the plot's already in mine head.
    Here they are.

    Enter BALTHAZAR *and* LORENZO.

BALTHAZAR.   How now Hieronimo,
    What, courting Bel-imperia?

HIERONIMO.   Ay my lord,
    Such courting as I promise you
    She hath my heart, but you my lord have hers.   55

LORENZO. But now, Hieronimo, or never,
    We are to entreat your help.

HIERONIMO.   My help,
    Why my good lords assure yourselves of me,
    For you have given me cause,
    Ay by my faith have you.

BALTHAZAR.   It pleased you   60
　　At the entertainment of the Ambassador,
　　To grace the King so much as with a show,
　　Now were your study so well furnished,
　　As for the passing of the first night's sport,
　　To entertain my father with the like: 65
　　Or any such like pleasing motion,
　　Assure yourself it would content them well.

HIERONIMO. Is this all?

BALTHAZAR. Ay, this is all.

HIERONIMO. Why then I'll fit you, say no more.   70
　　When I was young I gave my mind,
　　And plied myself to fruitless poetry:
　　Which though it profit the professor naught,
　　Yet is it passing pleasing to the world.

LORENZO. And how for that?

HIERONIMO.   Marry my good lord thus.   75
　　And yet methinks you are too quick with us.
　　When in Toledo there I studied,
　　It was my chance to write a tragedy,
　　See here my lords,

He shows them a book.

　　Which long forgot, I found this other day.   80
　　Now would your lordships favour me so much,
　　As but to grace me with your acting it,
　　I mean each one of you to play a part,
　　Assure you it will prove most passing strange,
　　And wondrous plausible to that assembly.   85

BALTHAZAR. What, would you have us play a tragedy?

HIERONIMO. Why Nero thought it no disparagement,
　　And kings and emperors have ta'en delight,
　　To make experience of their wits in plays?

LORENZO. Nay be not angry good Hieronimo,   90
　　The Prince but asked a question.

BALTHAZAR. In faith Hieronimo and you be in earnest,
  I'll make one.

LORENZO. And I another.

HIERONIMO. Now my good lord, could you entreat   95
  Your sister Bel-imperia to make one,
  For what's a play without a woman in it?

BEL-IMPERIA. Little entreaty shall serve me Hieronimo,
  For I must needs be employ'd in your play.

HIERONIMO. Why this is well, I tell you lordings,   100
  It was determin'd to have been acted
  By gentlemen and scholars too,
  Such as could tell what to speak.

BALTHAZAR. And now it shall be play'd by princes and courtiers,
  Such as can tell how to speak: 105
  If as it is our country manner,
  You will but let us know the argument.

HIERONIMO. That shall I roundly: the chronicles of Spain
  Record this written of a knight of Rhodes,
  He was betroth'd, and wedded at the length,   110
  To one Perseda an Italian dame,
  Whose beauty ravish'd all that her beheld,
  Especially the soul of Soliman,
  Who at the marriage was the chiefest guest.
  By sundry means sought Soliman to win   115
  Perseda's love, and could not gain the same.
  Then gan he break his passions to a friend,
  One of his bashaws whom he held full dear.
  Her had this bashaw long solicited,
  And saw she was not otherwise to be won,   120
  But by her husband's death this knight of Rhodes,
  Whom presently by treachery he slew.
  She stirr'd with an exceeding hate therefore,
  As cause of this slew Soliman.
  And to escape the bashaw's tyranny,   125
  Did stab herself, and this the tragedy.

LORENZO. O excellent!

BEL-IMPERIA.   But say Hieronimo
  What then became of him that was the bashaw?

HIERONIMO. Marry thus, mov'd with remorse of his misdeeds
  Ran to a mountain top and hung himself.   130

BALTHAZAR. But which of us is to perform that part?

HIERONIMO. O, that will I my lords, make no doubt of it,
  I'll play the murderer I warrant you,
  For I already have conceited that.

BALTHAZAR. And what shall I?   135

HIERONIMO. Great Soliman the Turkish Emperor.

LORENZO. And I?

HIERONIMO. Erastus the knight of Rhodes.

BEL-IMPERIA. And I?

HIERONIMO. Perseda, chaste and resolute.   140
  And here my lords are several abstracts drawn,
  For each of you to note your parts,
  And act it as occasion's offer'd you.
  You must provide a Turkish cap,
  A black mustachio and a fauchion.   145

Gives a paper to BALTHAZAR.

You with a cross like to a knight of Rhodes.

Gives another to LORENZO.

And madame, you must attire yourself,

He giveth BEL-IMPERIA *another.*

Like Phoebe, Flora, or the huntress,
Which to your discretion shall seem best.
And as for me my lords I'll look to one,   150
And with the ransom that the Viceroy sent,
So furnish and perform this tragedy,

As all the world shall say Hieronimo
Was liberal in gracing of it so.

BALTHAZAR. Hieronimo, methinks a comedy were better.   155

HIERONIMO. A comedy,
   Fie, comedies are fit for common wits
   But to present a kingly troupe withal,
   Give me a stately written tragedy.
   Tragedia cothurnata, fitting kings,   160
   Containing matter, and not common things.
   My lords, all this must be perform'd,
   As fitting for the first night's revelling.
   The Italian tragedians were so sharp of wit,
   That in one hour's meditation,   165
   They would perform anything in action.

LORENZO. And well it may, for I have seen the like
   In Paris, 'mongst the French tragedians.

HIERONIMO. In Paris, mass and well remembered,
   There's one thing more that rests for us to do.   170

BALTHAZAR. What's that Hieronimo, forget not anything.

HIERONIMO. Each one of us must act his part
   In unknown languages,
   That it may breed the more variety.
   As you my lord in Latin, I in Greek,   175
   You in Italian, and for because I know,
   That Bel-imperia hath practised the French,
   In courtly French shall all her phrases be.

BEL-IMPERIA. You mean to try my cunning then Hieronimo.

BALTHAZAR. But this will be a mere confusion,   180
   And hardly shall we all be understood.

HIERONIMO. It must be so, for the conclusion
   Shall prove the invention, and all was good:
   And I myself in an oration,
   And with a strange and wondrous show besides,   185
   That I will have there behind a curtain,

Assure yourself shall make the matter known.
And all shall be concluded in one scene,
For there's no pleasure ta'en in tediousness.

BALTHAZAR [*aside, to* LORENZO]. How like you this?   190

LORENZO. Why, thus my lord,
We must resolve to soothe his humours up.

BALTHAZAR. On then Hieronimo, farewell till soon.

HIERONIMO. You'll ply this gear.

LORENZO.   I warrant you.

Exeunt all but HIERONIMO.

HIERONIMO. Why so, now shall I see the fall of Babylon,   195
Wrought by the heavens in this confusion.
And if the world like not this tragedy,
Hard is the hap of old Hieronimo.

Exit.

Act IV, Scene ii

Enter ISABELLA *with a weapon.*

ISABELLA. Tell me no more, O monstrous homicides,
Since neither piety nor pity moves
The King to justice or compassion:
I will revenge myself upon this place,
Where thus they murdered my beloved son.   5

She cuts down the arbour.

Down with these branches and these loathsome boughs,
Of this unfortunate and fatal pine.
Down with them Isabella, rent them up,
And burn the roots from whence the rest is sprung:
I will not leave a root, a stalk, a tree,   10
A bough, a branch, a blossom, nor a leaf,
No, not an herb within this garden plot.

Accursed complot of my misery,
Fruitless for ever may this garden be.
Barren the earth, and blissless whosoever   15
Imagines not to keep it unmanur'd:
An eastern wind commix'd with noisome airs
Shall blast the plants and the young saplings,
The earth with serpents shall be pestered,
And passengers for fear to be infect,   20
Shall stand aloof, and, looking at it, tell
'There murd'red died the son of Isabel.'
Ay here he died, and here I him embrace,
See where his ghost solicits with his wounds,
Revenge on her that should revenge his death.   25
Hieronimo, make haste to see thy son,
For sorrow and despair hath cited me,
To hear Horatio plead with Rhadamanth.
Make haste, Hieronimo to hold excus'd
Thy negligence in pursuit of their deaths,   30
Whose hateful wrath bereav'd him of his breath.
Ah nay, thou dost delay their deaths,
Forgives the murderers of thy noble son,
And none but I bestir me, to no end,
And as I curse this tree from further fruit,   35
So shall my womb be cursed for his sake,
And with this weapon will I wound the breast,
The hapless breast that gave Horatio suck.

She stabs herself.

Act IV, Scene iii

Enter HIERONIMO, *he knocks up the curtain. Enter the Duke of* CASTILE.

CASTILE. How now Hieronimo where's your fellows,
    That you take all this pain?

HIERONIMO. O sir, it is for the author's credit,
    To look that all things may go well:
    But good my lord let me entreat your grace   5
    To give the king the copy of the play:
    This is the argument of what we show.

CASTILE. I will Hieronimo.

HIERONIMO. One thing more my good lord.

CASTILE. What's that?   10

HIERONIMO. Let me entreat your grace,
    That when the train are pass'd into the gallery,
    You would vouchsafe to throw me down the key.

CASTILE. I will Hieronimo.

    Exit CASTILE.

HIERONIMO. What are you ready Balthazar?   15
    Bring a chair and a cushion for the King.

    Enter BALTHAZAR *with a chair.*

    Well done Balthazar, hang up the title.
    Our scene is Rhodes. What, is your beard on?

BALTHAZAR. Half on, the other is in my hand.

HIERONIMO. Despatch for shame, are you so long?   20

    Exit BALTHAZAR.

    Bethink thyself Hieronimo,
    Recall thy wits, recompt thy former wrongs
    Thou has receiv'd by murder of thy son.
    And lastly, not least, how Isabel,
    Once his mother and thy dearest wife,   25
    All woebegone for him hath slain herself.
    Behoves thee then Hieronimo to be reveng'd.
    The plot is laid of dire revenge,
    On then Hieronimo, pursue revenge,
    For nothing wants but acting of revenge.   30

    Exit HIERONIMO.

Act IV, Scene iv

Enter Spanish KING, VICEROY, *the Duke of* CASTILE, *and their train.*

KING. Now Viceroy, shall we see the tragedy
    Of Soliman the Turkish Emperor:
    Perform'd of pleasure by your son the Prince,
    My nephew Don Lorenzo, and my niece.

VICEROY. Who, Bel-imperia?   5

KING. Ay, and Hieronimo our Marshal,
    At whose request they deign to do 't themselves.
    These be our pastimes in the Court of Spain.
    Here brother, you shall be the book-keeper.
    This is the argument of that they show.   10

He giveth him a book.

Gentlemen, this play of Hieronimo in sundry languages,
was thought good to be set down in English more largely,
for the easier understanding to every public reader.

Enter BALTHAZAR, BEL-IMPERIA, *and* HIERONIMO.

BALTHAZAR. Bashaw, that Rhodes is ours, yield heavens
    the honour,
    And holy Mahomet, our sacred prophet:
    And be thou grac'd with every excellence
    That Soliman can give, or thou desire.
    But thy desert in conquering Rhodes is less,   15
    Than in reserving this fair Christian nymph
    Perseda, blissful lamp of excellence:
    Whose eyes compel like powerful adamant,
    The warlike heart of Soliman to wait.

KING. See Viceroy, that is Balthazar your son,   20
    That represents the emperor Soliman:
    How well he acts his amorous passion.

VICEROY. Ay Bel-imperia hath taught him that.

CASTILE. That's because his mind runs all on Bel-imperia.   24

HIERONIMO. Whatever joy earth yields betide your majesty.

BALTHAZAR. Earth yields no joy without Perseda's love.

HIERONIMO. Let then Perseda on your grace attend.

BALTHAZAR. She shall not wait on me, but I on her,
Drawn by the influence of her lights, I yield.
But let my friend the Rhodian knight come forth,   30
Erasto, dearer than my life to me,
That he may see Perseda my beloved.

Enter LORENZO [*as* ERASTO].

KING. Here comes Lorenzo, look upon the plot,
And tell me brother what part plays he?

BEL-IMPERIA. Ah my Erasto, welcome to Perseda.   35

LORENZO. Thrice happy is Erasto, that thou liv'st,
Rhodes' loss is nothing to Erasto's joy:
Sith his Perseda lives, his life survives.

BALTHAZAR. Ah bashaw, here is love between Erasto
And fair Perseda sovereign of my soul.   40

HIERONIMO. Remove Erasto mighty Soliman,
And then Perseda will be quickly won.

BALTHAZAR. Erasto is my friend, and while he lives,
Perseda never will remove her love

HIERONIMO. Let not Erasto live, to grieve great Soliman.   45

BALTHAZAR. Dear is Erasto in our princely eye.

HIERONIMO. But if he be your rival, let him die.

BALTHAZAR. Why let him die, so love commandeth me.
Yet grieve I that Erasto should so die.

HIERONIMO. Erasto, Soliman saluteth thee,   50
And lets thee wit by me his highness' will:
Which is, thou shouldst be thus employ'd.

Stab him.

BEL-IMPERIA.   Ay me
    Erasto, see Soliman, Erasto's slain.

BALTHAZAR. Yet liveth Soliman to comfort thee.
    Fair queen of beauty, let not favour die,   55
    But with a gracious eye behold his grief,
    That with Perseda's beauty is increas'd,
    If by Perseda's grief be not releas'd.

BEL-IMPERIA. Tyrant, desist soliciting vain suits,
    Relentless are mine ears to thy laments,   60
    As thy butcher is pitiless and base,
    Which seiz'd on my Erasto, harmless knight.
    Yet by thy power thou thinkest to command,
    And to thy power Perseda doth obey:
    But were she able, thus she would revenge   65
    Thy treacheries on thee, ignoble Prince:

Stab him.

    And on herself she would be thus reveng'd.

Stab herself.

KING. Well said old Marshal, this was bravely done.

HIERONIMO. But Bel-imperia plays Perseda well.

VICEROY. Were this in earnest Bel-imperia,   70
    You would be better to my son than so.

KING. But now what follows for Hieronimo?

HIERONIMO. Marry this follows for Hieronimo.
    Here break we off our sundry languages,
    And thus conclude I in our vulgar tongue.   75
    Haply you think, but bootless are your thoughts,
    That this is fabulously counterfeit,
    And that we do as all tragedians do:
    To die today (for fashioning our scene)
    The death of Ajax, or some Roman peer,   80
    And in a minute starting up again,
    Revive to please tomorrow's audience.

No, Princes, know I am Hieronimo,
The hopeless father of a hapless son,
Whose tongue is tun'd to tell his latest tale,   85
Not to excuse gross errors in the play.
I see your looks urge instance of these words,
Behold the reason urging me to this.

Shows his dead son.

See here my show, look on this spectacle:
Here lay my hope, and here my hope hath end: 90
Here lay my heart, and here my heart was slain:
Here lay my treasure, here my treasure lost:
Here lay my bliss, and here my bliss bereft.
But hope, heart, treasure, joy, and bliss:
All fled, fail'd, died, yea all decay'd with this.   95
From forth these wounds came breath that gave me life,
They murd'red me that made these fatal marks:
The cause was love, whence grew this mortal hate,
The hate, Lorenzo and young Balthazar:
The love, my son to Bel-imperia.   100
But night the coverer of accursed crimes,
With pitchy silence hush'd these traitors' harms,
And lent them leave, for they had sorted leisure,
To take advantage in my garden plot,
Upon my son, my dear Horatio: 105
There merciless they butcher'd up my boy,
In black dark night, to pale dim cruel death.
He shrieks, I heard, and yet methinks I hear,
His dismal outcry echo in the air:
With soonest speed I hasted to the noise,   110
Where hanging on a tree, I found my son,
Through girt with wounds, and slaught'red as you see.
And griev'd I (think you) at this spectacle?
Speak, Portuguese, whose loss resembles mine,
If thou canst weep upon thy Balthazar,   115
'Tis like I wail'd for my Horatio.
And you my lord whose reconciled son
March'd in a net, and thought himself unseen,

And rated me for brainsick lunacy,
With 'God amend that mad Hieronimo',   120
How can you brook our play's catastrophe?
And here behold this bloody hand-kercher,
Which at Horatio's death I weeping dipp'd
Within the river of his bleeding wounds.
It as propitious, see I have reserv'd,   125
And never hath it left my bloody heart,
Soliciting remembrance of my vow.
With these, O these accursed murderers,
Which now perform'd, my heart is satisfied.
And to this end the bashaw I became,   130
That might revenge me on Lorenzo's life,
Who therefore was appointed to the part,
And was to represent the knight of Rhodes,
That I might kill him more conveniently.
So Viceroy was this Balthazar thy son,   135
That Soliman, which Bel-imperia
In person of Perseda murdered:
Solely appointed to that tragic part,
That she might slay him that offended her.
Poor Bel-imperia miss'd her part in this,   140
For though the story saith she should have died,
Yet I of kindness, and of care to her,
Did otherwise determine of her end.
But love of him whom they did hate too much
Did urge her resolution to be such.   145
And Princes now behold Hieronimo,
Author and actor in this tragedy,
Bearing his latest fortune in his fist:
And will as resolute conclude his part,
As any of the actors gone before.   150
And gentles, thus I end my play,
Urge no more words, I have no more to say.

He runs to hang himself.

KING. O hearken Viceroy, hold Hieronimo.
Brother, my nephew, and thy son are slain.

VICEROY. We are betray'd, my Balthazar is slain,   155
    Break ope the doors, run save Hieronimo.

[HIERONIMO *is brought back, guarded.*]

    Hieronimo, do but inform the King of these events,
    Upon mine honour thou shalt have no harm.

HIERONIMO. Viceroy, I will not trust thee with my life,
    Which I this day have offered to my son: 160
    Accursed wretch,
    Why stayest thou him that was resolv'd to die?

KING. Speak traitor, damned, bloody murderer speak,
    For now I have thee I will make thee speak:
    Why hast thou done this undeserving deed?   165

VICEROY. Why hast thou murdered my Balthazar?

CASTILE. Why hast thou butchered both my children thus?

HIERONIMO. O good words,
    As dear to me was my Horatio,
    As yours, or yours, or yours my lord to you.   170
    My guiltless son was by Lorenzo slain,
    And by Lorenzo and that Balthazar,
    And I at last revenged thoroughly.
    Upon whose souls may heavens be yet aveng'd,
    With greater far than these afflictions.   175

CASTILE. But who were thy confederates in this?

VICEROY. That was thy daughter Bel-imperia.
    For by her hand my Balthazar was slain.
    I saw her stab him.

KING.   Why speak'st thou not?

HIERONIMO. What lesser liberty can kings afford   180
    Than harmless silence? Then afford it me:
    Sufficeth I may not, nor I will not tell thee.

KING. Fetch forth the tortures.
    Traitor as thou art, I'll make thee tell.

HIERONIMO.   Indeed,
   Thou may'st torment me as his wretched son   185
   Hath done in murdering my Horatio.
   But never shalt thou force me to reveal
   The thing which I have vow'd inviolate:
   And therefore in despite of all thy threats,
   Pleas'd with their deaths, and eas'd with their revenge: 190
   First take my tongue, and afterwards my heart.

[He bites off his tongue.]

KING. O monstrous resolution of a wretch,
   See Viceroy, he hath bitten forth his tongue,
   Rather than to reveal what we requir'd.

CASTILE. Yet can he write.   195

KING. And if in this he satisfy us not,
   We will devise th' extremest kind of death
   That ever was invented for a wretch.

Then [HIERONIMO] *makes signs for a knife to mend his pen.*

CASTILE. O he would have a knife to mend his pen.

VICEROY. Here, and advise thee that thou write the troth.   200
   Look to my brother, save Hieronimo.

[HIERONIMO] *with a knife stabs the* DUKE *and himself.*

KING. What age hath ever heard such monstrous deeds?
   My brother and the whole succeeding hope,
   That Spain expected after my decease.
   Go bear his body hence that we may mourn   205
   The loss of our beloved brother's death,
   That he may be entomb'd what e'er befall,
   I am the next, the nearest, last of all.

VICEROY. And thou Don Pedro do the like for us,
   Take up our hapless son untimely slain: 210
   Set me with him, and he with woeful me,
   Upon the main mast of a ship unmann'd,
   And let the wind and tide haul me along,

To Scylla's barking and untamed grief:
Or to the loathsome pool of Acheron,   215
To weep my want for my sweet Balthazar,
Spain hath no refuge for a Portingale.

The trumpets sound a dead march, the KING *of Spain mourning after his brother's body, and the* VICEROY *of Portingale bearing the body of his son.*

Act IV, Scene v

GHOST [*of Andrea*] *and* REVENGE.

ANDREA. Ay, now my hopes have end in their effects,
    When blood and sorrow finish my desires:
    Horatio murdered in his father's bower,
    Vild Serberine by Pedringano slain,
    False Pedringano hang'd by quaint device,   5
    Fair Isabella by herself misdone,
    Prince Balthazar by Bel-imperia stabb'd,
    The Duke of Castile and his wicked son,
    Both done to death by old Hieronimo,
    My Bel-imperia fall'n as Dido fell,   10
    And good Hieronimo slain by himself:
    Ay these were spectacles to please my soul.
    Now will I beg at lovely Proserpine,
    That by the virtue of her princely doom,
    I may consort my friends in pleasing sort,   15
    And on my foes work just and sharp revenge.
    I'll lead my friend Horatio through those fields,
    Where never dying wars are still inur'd.
    I'll lead fair Isabella to that train,
    Where pity weeps but never feeleth pain.   20
    I'll lead my Bel-imperia to those joys,
    That vestal virgins, and fair queens possess.
    I'll lead Hieronimo where Orpheus plays,
    Adding sweet pleasure to eternal days.

But say Revenge, for thou must help or none,   25
    Against the rest how shall my hate be shown?

REVENGE. This hand shall hale them down to deepest hell,
    Where none but furies, bugs and tortures dwell.

ANDREA. Then sweet Revenge do this at my request,
    Let me be judge and doom them to unrest.   30
    Let loose poor Tityus from the vulture's gripe,
    And let Don Cyprian supply his room,
    Place Don Lorenzo on Ixion's wheel,
    And let the lover's endless pains surcease:
    Juno forgets old wrath and grants him ease.   35
    Hang Balthazar about Chimaera's neck,
    And let him there bewail his bloody love,
    Repining at our joys that are above.
    Let Serberine go roll the fatal stone,
    And take from Sisyphus his endless moan.   40
    False Pedringano for his treachery,
    Let him be dragg'd through boiling Acheron,
    And there live dying still in endless flames,
    Blaspheming gods and all their holy names.   44

REVENGE. Then haste we down to meet thy friends and foes,
    To place thy friends in ease, the rest in woes.
    For here, though death hath end their misery,
    I'll there begin their endless tragedy.

    Exeunt.

Appendix: the Painter's Scene

This, the fourth and most extensive of the Additions included in the edition of 1602, is located between Act III, Scenes xii and xiii, the final stage direction replacing the first of the present Scene xiii.

Enter JAQUES *and* PEDRO.

JAQUES. I wonder Pedro why our master thus
    At midnight sends us with our torches' light,
    When man and bird and beast are all at rest,
    Save those that watch for rape and bloody murder.

PEDRO. O Jaques, know thou that our master's mind   5
    Is much distraught since his Horatio died,
    And now his aged years should sleep in rest,
    His heart in quiet, like a desperate man,
    Grows lunatic and childish for his son:
    Sometimes, as he doth at his table sit,   10
    He speaks as if Horatio stood by him,
    Then starting in a rage falls on the earth,
    Cries out, 'Horatio, where is my Horatio?'
    So that with extreme grief and cutting sorrow,
    There is not left in him one inch of man.   15
    See where he comes.

Enter HIERONIMO.

HIERONIMO. I pry through every crevice of each wall,
    Look on each tree, and search through every brake,
    Beat at the bushes, stamp our grandam earth,
    Dive in the water, and stare up to heaven,   20
    Yet cannot I behold my son Horatio.
    How now, who's there, sprites, sprites?

PEDRO. We are your servants that attend you, sir.

HIERONIMO. What make you with your torches in the dark?

PEDRO. You bid us light them, and attend you here.   25

HIERONIMO. No, no, you are deceiv'd, not I, you are deceiv'd:
    Was I so mad to bid you light your torches now?
    Light me your torches at the mid of noon,
    Whenas the sun-god rides in all his glory:
    Light me your torches then.

PEDRO.   Then we burn daylight.   30

HIERONIMO. Let it be burnt. Night is a murderous slut,
    That would not have her treasons to be seen;
    And yonder pale-faced Hecate there, the moon,
    Doth give consent to that is done in darkness;
    And all those stars that gaze upon her face,   35
    Are aglets on her sleeve, pins on her train;
    And those that should be powerful and divine,
    Do sleep in darkness when they most should shine.

PEDRO. Provoke them not, fair sir, with tempting words:
    The heavens are gracious, and your miseries   40
    And sorrow makes you speak you know not what.

HIERONIMO. Villain, thou liest, and thou doest naught
    But tell me I am mad: thou liest, I am not mad.
    I know thee to be Pedro, and he Jaques.
    I'll prove it to thee, and were I mad, how could I?   45
    Where was she that same night when my Horatio
    Was murdered? She should have shone: search thou the book.
    Had the moon shone, in my boy's face there was a kind of grace,
    That I know (nay, I do know) had the murderer seen him,
    His weapon would have fall'n and cut the earth,   50
    Had he been fram'd of naught but blood and death.
    Alack, when mischief doth it knows not what,
    What shall we say to mischief?

    Enter ISABELLA.

ISABELLA. Dear Hieronimo, come in a-doors.
    O seek not means so to increase thy sorrow.   55

HIERONIMO. Indeed Isabella we do nothing here.
    I do not cry, ask Pedro, and ask Jaques:
    Not I indeed, we are very merry, very merry.

ISABELLA. How? Be merry here, be merry here?
    Is not this the place, and this the very tree,   60
    Where my Horatio died, where he was murdered?

HIERONIMO. Was – do not say what: let her weep it out.
    This was the tree, I set it of a kernel,
    And when our hot Spain could not let it grow,
    But that the infant and the human sap   65
    Began to wither, duly twice a morning
    Would I be sprinkling it with fountain water.
    At last it grew, and grew, and bore and bore,
    Till at length
    It grew a gallows, and did bear our son.   70
    It bore thy fruit and mine. O wicked, wicked plant.

One knocks within at the door.

See who knock there.

PEDRO.   It is a painter, sir.

HIERONIMO. Bid him come in, and paint some comfort,
For surely there's none lives but painted comfort.
Let him come in. One knows not what may chance.   75
God's will that I should set this tree – but even so
Masters ungrateful servants rear from naught,
And then they hate them that did bring them up.

Enter the PAINTER.

PAINTER. God bless you, sir.

HIERONIMO. Wherefore? Why, thou scornful villain,   80
How, where, or by what means should I be bless'd?

ISABELLA. What wouldst thou have, good fellow?

PAINTER. Justice, madam.

HIERONIMO. O ambitious beggar, wouldst thou have that
That lives not in the world?
Why, all the undelved mines cannot buy   85
An ounce of justice, 'tis a jewel so inestimable:
I tell thee,
God hath engross'd all justice in his hands,
And there is none, but what comes from him.

PAINTER. O then I see   90
That God must right me for my murdered son.

HIERONIMO. How, was thy son murdered?

PAINTER. Ay sir, no man did hold a son so dear.

HIERONIMO. What, not as thine? That's a lie
As messy as the earth: I had a son,   95
Whose least unvalued hair did weigh
A thousand of thy sons: and he was murdered.

PAINTER. Alas sir, I had no more but he.

HIERONIMO. Nor I, nor I, but this same one of mine
Was worth a legion: but all is one.   100
Pedro, Jaques, go in a-doors: Isabella go,
And this good fellow here and I
Will range this hideous orchard up and down,
Like to two lions reaved of their young.
Go in a-doors, I say.   105

Exeunt [ISABELLA, PEDRO, JAQUES]. *The* PAINTER *and he sits down.*

Come, let's talk wisely now. Was thy son murdered?

PAINTER. Ay sir.

HIERONIMO. So was mine. How dost take it? Art thou not sometimes mad?
Is there no tricks that comes before thine eyes?

PAINTER. O Lord, yes sir. 110

HIERONIMO. Art a painter? Canst paint me a tear, or a wound,
a groan or a sigh? Canst paint me such a tree as this?

PAINTER. Sir, I am sure you have heard of my painting, my name's Bazardo.

HIERONIMO. Bazardo! Afore God, an excellent fellow. Look you sir, 115
do you see, I'd have you paint me in my gallery, in your oil colours
matted, and draw me five years younger than I am. Do you see sir,
let five years go, let them go, like the Marshal of Spain. My wife
Isabella standing by me, with a speaking look to my son Horatio,
which should intend to this or some such like purpose: 'God 120
bless thee, my sweet son.' And my hand leaning upon his head,
thus sir, do you see? May it be done?

PAINTER. Very well sir.

HIERONIMO. Nay, I pray mark me sir. Then sir, would I have you
paint me this tree, this very tree. Canst paint a doleful cry? 125

PAINTER. Seemingly, sir.

HIERONIMO. Nay, it should cry: but all is one. Well sir, paint me a
youth run through and through with villains' swords, hanging upon
this tree. Canst thou draw a murderer?

PAINTER. I'll warrant you sir, I have the pattern of the most 130
notorious villains that ever lived in all Spain.

HIERONIMO. O, let them be worse, worse: stretch thine art, and let
their beards be of Judas his own colour, and let their eyebrows jutty
over: in any case observe that. Then sir, after some violent noise,
bring me forth in my shirt, and my gown under mine arm, with 135
my torch in my hand, and my sword reared up thus: and with these
words: 'What noise is this? Who calls Hieronimo?' May it be done?

PAINTER. Yea sir.

HIERONIMO. Well sir, then bring me forth, bring me through alley
and alley, still with a distracted countenance going along, and let 140
my hair heave up my night-cap. Let the clouds scowl, make the
moon dark, the stars extinct, the winds blowing, the bells tolling,

the owl shrieking, the toads croaking, the minutes jarring, and the
clock striking twelve. And then at last, sir, starting, behold a man
hanging and tottering and tottering, as you know the wind will   145
weave a man, and I with a trice to cut him down. And looking
upon him by the advantage of my torch, find it to be my son
Horatio. There you may show a passion, there you may show a
passion. Draw me like old Priam of Troy, crying 'The house is
afire, the house is afire as the torch over my head.' Make me   150
curse, make me rave, make me cry, make me mad, make me
well again, make me curse hell, invocate heaven, and in the end,
leave me in a trance: and so forth.

PAINTER. And is this the end?

HIERONIMO. O no, there is no end: the end is death and madness.   155
As I am never better than when I am mad, then methinks I am
a brave fellow, then I do wonders: but reason abuseth me, and
there's the torment, there's the hell. At the last, sir, bring me to
one of the murderers, were he as strong as Hector, thus would
I tear and drag him up and down.   160

He beats the PAINTER *in, then comes out again with a book in his hand.*

Glossary

Acheron – river of the underworld

adamant – diamond with magnetic properties, loadstone

advantage, small – here, an insignificant flaw

Aeacus – one of the three judges of the underworld

Aetna – volcanic mountain in Sicily

aglets – ornamental tags on laces, spangles on a dress

Alcides – Hercules, one of whose 'labours' was to bind up Cerberus in the underworld

ambages – circuitous, evasive speeches

argument – at IV, i, 107: outline of a plot

Ariadne's twines – like the threads used by Ariadne to guide Theseus out of the labyrinth

Avernus – lake near Naples, traditionally close to the entrance to the underworld

band – bond

bane – poison

bashaw – high-ranking Turkish nobleman

Bellona – goddess of war

bewray – betray, reveal

book-keeper – in a theatrical context, as here, the prompter

boot – advantage, compensation

break – at IV, i, 117: reveal, lay bare

Cerberus – three-headed dog, guardian of the underworld

Charon – ferryman of the dead in the underworld

Che le Ieron – a phrase in pastiche Italian without clear meaning

Chimaera – fire-breathing beast

cited – summoned

close with one – attack somebody at close quarters

coil – fuss, nuisance

complot – conspiracy

conceits – ingenious ideas, jokes

condescent – assent, permission

corlonel – old pronunciation of 'colonel'

cornet – company of cavalry

corregidor – Spanish magistrate, but presumably Kyd means an advocate here

corsive – corrosive: wearing away at

countermur'd – doubly-walled

courser – swift horse

dag – pistol

ding'd – threw

distain'd – stained, sullied

doom, censure of my – 'consequence of my judgement'

ejectione firma – a writ of ejection from a tenanted property

enlarg'd – given her freedom

Erichtho – Thessalian sorceress

Est tremulo . . . proditionis opus – 'Craven fear they joined to dismayed dread – a foolish, fruitless treachery' (Latin)

Et quel . . . mi bassara – 'And what I want, no-one knows. So long as I understand it, that's enough!' (Italian)

exclaims – exclamations, cries

Fata . . . habes sepulchrum – the following two lines (III, xiii, 14-15) give Hieronimo's own paraphrase of Seneca's Latin

fatch, reaching – far-sighted idea

fauchion – broad sword, curved in the Turkish fashion

Flora – goddess of flowers and of fertility

gage – pledge

gear – business, matter in hand

girt, through – pierced from all sides

guerdon – reward

hale – drag

haps, good – good fortune

hight – was called

holp – helped

Horn, Gates of – one of the twin 'gates of sleep', from which true visions emerge

huntress – at IV, i, 148: Diana, goddess of hunting

Hymen – god of marriage (but here ominously dressed in black)

interdicted – forbidden

Ixion – mythical lover of Hera, punished by turning on a wheel for eternity

leese – lose

list not – have no wish to

loadstar – a star to set a ship's course by

Marsyas – satyr punished for challenging Apollo's skill in flute-playing

mean, think upon a – devise a way

meed – reward

messy – massive, huge

Mi. Chi mi fa . . . otrada vule – 'He who unexpectedly befriends me means to betray me' (Italian)

Minos – one of the three judges of the underworld, who held the casting vote

misconster – misconstrue, deliberately misinterpret

moiety – equal share

myrmidons – the warriors attendant upon Achilles

Nemesis – goddess of revenge

nill – will not

O aliquis mihi . . . nulla sequatur –
'Let the fine herbs of spring
be gathered for me, / Lay on
a soothing balm, a salve to
grief: / If such be known,
let juices of oblivion be
brought. / I myself will
gather from the corners of
the world / Whatever herbs
the sun draws to the light. /
I myself will drink such
potions as wise women can
devise, / Whatever herbs
their secret incantations can
bring forth. /
I will attempt all things,
even death, / Until all
feeling is extinguished from
my heart. / Shall I never
again in life see those eyes, /
That light of life snuffed out
in endless sleep? / To die
with you would make a joy
the journey to the shades
below, / But I must keep
from such a hastened end, /
Lest your own death goes
unrevenged.' (This pastiche
Latin sonnet is
of Kyd's own devising, a
patchwork of borrowed
phrases and invention)

O multum . . . victoria juris – 'O
beloved of God, for you –
fought over by the heavens
and worshipped by the
peoples of the earth –
victory is sister to

righteousness' (from the
classical poet Claudian)

Orpheus – in Greek mythology,
Thracian poet who so
charmed Persephone with
his music that she allowed
his dead wife Eurydice to
follow him from the
underworld

Pallas – protective goddess of
the Athenians, especially
against Troy

Pan – god of shepherds, who
unwisely dared to challenge
Apollo's skill in flute-playing

paunch'd – stabbed in the belly

Pede pes . . . petiturque viro – 'Foot
opposed to foot, spear to
spear, weapon against
weapon, man against man'
(Latin, source uncertain)

Per scelus . . . sceleribus iter –
'Crime must be made safe
through further crime'
(Latin, adapted from Seneca)

Pergamus – city close to Troy,
and here associated with
its fall

Phlegethon – a river of the
underworld, with waves
of fire

Phoebe – goddess of the moon

pitch'd – agreed

plain me – complain

Pluto – ruler of the underworld

Pocas palabras – a few words
(Spanish)

poniard – dagger

professor – here, one who professes or practices (in this case, poetry)

Proserpine – wife to Pluto, and so queen of the underworld

puissant – powerful

Qui jacet . . . obesse magis – 'Who lies on the earth can fall no further, and Fortune has no power to injure more: nothing can harm me now' (Latin)

rampiers – ramparts

reaved – bereaved, robbed

reck – reckon, attend to

Remedium malorum iners est – 'is a powerless antidote to evil' (Latin, from Seneca)

Rhadamanth – one of the three judges of the underworld

room, supply his – take his place

scutcheon – shield bearing a coat of arms

seld – seldom

shifts – tricks, stratagems

Sisyphus – legendary King of Crete, condemned to roll a stone uphill for eternity

sith – since

stand you – 'if you rely on' (while he also 'stands' on the hangman's trap)

surcease – cease

Tam . . . ingenio – 'Equally by force and ingenuity'

Terceira – Portuguese possession in the Azores: hence, the conqueror of any newly-discovered land

Thetis – daughter of the sea god: here, the sea itself

Thracian poet – Orpheus

tickle point – finely balanced ('ticklish') point

Tityus – giant condemned in eternity to endure two vultures feeding on his liver

Tragedia cothurnata – tragedy performed in the *cothurnus*, or elevated boot, which signified the form in ancient Athens

Vien qui presto – 'Come here quickly'

vild – vile

Vindicta mihi – 'Vengeance is mine (I will repay, saith the Lord', as this biblical injunction against private revenge continues)

ward, watch and – keep guard

watch – band of citizens appointed to keep the peace at night

water breach – leakage (as here, in a breached dyke)

whilom – once, formerly

whipstalk – whip, presumably as used to spin a top

wit – at IV, iii, 51: know

wot – know